THE PHILOSOPHY OF SCIENCE, AND ECONOMICS

D0169270

Also by Robert A. Solo

ECONOMICS AND THE PUBLIC INTEREST *(editor)*
ECONOMIC ORGANIZATIONS AND SOCIAL SYSTEMS
ESSAI SUR L'AMERIQUE
INDUCING TECHNOLOGICAL CHANGE FOR ECONOMIC
GROWTH AND DEVELOPMENT *(co-editor with Everett Rogers)*
ORGANIZING SCIENCE FOR TECHNOLOGY TRANSFER IN
ECONOMIC DEVELOPMENT
ACROSS THE HIGH TECHNOLOGY THRESHOLD
THE POLITICAL AUTHORITY AND THE MARKET SYSTEM
THE POSITIVE STATE
VALUE JUDGMENTS AND INCOME DISTRIBUTION
(co-editor with Charles Anderson)
OPPORTUNITY KNOCKS: AMERICAN ECONOMIC POLICY
AFTER GORBACHEV

The Philosophy of Science, and Economics

Robert A Solo

Emeritus Professor of Economics
Michigan State University, East Lansing

M. E. Sharpe, Inc.
Armonk, New York

First published in the United States in 1991 by M. E. Sharpe, Inc.
80 Business Park Drive, Armonk, New York 10504

Published in Great Britain by
Macmillan Academic and Professional Ltd

Printed in Great Britain

Library of Congress Cataloging-in-Publication Data
Solo, Robert A.
The philosophy of science, and economics / by Robert A. Solo.
p.   cm.
Includes bibliographical references and index.
ISBN 0–87332–899–X
1. Solo, Robert A.   2. Economists—United States—Biography.
3. Economics—Methodology.   4. Science—Philosophy.
5. Technological innovations–Economic aspects.   I. Title.
HB119.S65A3   1991
330.1—dc20
                                        91–23989
                                        CIP

To Rozie, Tova, Volodya and Rocky

Contents

1

Confessions

This chapter offers an introduction to and an apology for what I intend to write about here. It does so through a personal recollection of my discovery and exploration of facets in the idea of science, enlivened by some memories of persons and events encountered along the way.

While anything autobiographical risks irritating the reader with too much talk of self, it is an approach that at least will serve to put my arguments in perspective and to make clear my limited qualification for the task at hand.

Things went well for me at the start. I transferred to Harvard in 1936. In my two years there I learned to be an economist, and graduated in June 1938 at the top of my class in that field. I spent the academic year 1938–9 on a fellowship at the American University in Washington, DC, studying for an MA again in economics, working at odd jobs and waiting for the next civil service examination. Of the grades of the twelve thousand or so of those who took the junior professional examination that summer, mine was one of the top five. In the early Fall of 1939 I started as a junior member of a small 'brain trust' formed to assist Harry Hopkins in his role as adviser to President Roosevelt. Within that year I had published *Industrial Capacity in the United States*, and an article in *Econometrica*.

As war approached, I shifted to the War Production Board, and later was appointed Assistant to the American Executive Secretary of the Combined (British American) Raw Materials Board. When in the Spring of 1942 I left for training as a naval officer I had climbed the four regular grades to the top of the professional civil service, and my inflation-adjusted income was as high or higher than it

1

would ever be again. Before going overseas, I married the woman I had been living with in Washington. After years of service in the South and Central Pacific. I was demobilized in 1945. I had no desire to return to work in government, nor was I clear on what sort of career I should pursue. I decided to 'retool' under the GI Bill of Rights, and give myself a few years to find my way or to be carried along by the drift of events. In the late Fall of 1945 my wife and I embarked from New York on the old *Queen Mary*, bound for Southampton. That once great luxury liner, war weary and worn, had been reduced to the bare and shabby bones of a troopship. Beside the two of us there were on board only a small contingent of Britons returning from the battered outpost of Empire, uneasy at coming back to their tight class-bound society after the turmoil and mobility of war. As the one who stood in proxy for America, they blasted me daily for monopolizing the world's wealth, as though I had robbed them personally; and were disconcerted to discover that in spite of all the gold in Fort Knox, an American such as myself was at least as poor as they were.

We settled in the bombed out but vital city of London and both my wife and I enrolled to study for a doctorate in economics at the London School of Economics and Political Science (LSE). It is there that the story begins.

The doctoral programme at the London School of Economics was different than at any American university. There were no prescribed fields, no prelims, no required courses. There were numerous lecture series and seminars offered by the faculty and by a distinguished set of visiting academics. Attendance was voluntary, without examination or grades. A large monthly meeting brought together the whole of the economics faculty and graduate students for the presentation of a paper and an open discussion of it. Essentially the doctoral programme provided for the close supervision of the individual graduate student by a selected member of the faculty in preparing for and in writing the dissertation.

LIONEL ROBBINS AT THE LONDON SCHOOL OF ECONOMICS

My supervisor was the economist, Lionel (later Lord) Robbins, a tall, handsome Englishman of great charm and gentility. To me he seemed to epitomize the British country gentleman. Before returning to his professorship at LSE he had spent the war years with the Treasury at the higher reaches of the British civil service. Distinguished, internationally known, sure-footed in the realm of organizational politics, Robbins dominated the LSE. I liked Robbins and admired him, especially for the great breadth of his culture. And he liked me. He boasted of me to his colleagues; praising me to the skies. He was a wonderful patron and a good friend. If I had stayed in his good graces, my career would have been assured. He was also, as I would later discover, a ferocious and vindictive enemy. We got along swimmingly until the time came for me to select a dissertation topic.

And now I must deviate to confess an element of deceit in my position. I had gained a local notoriety as a child poet, sowing family expectations that I would someday become a 'writer'. Certainly I continued to demonstrate a proclivity with words, and my mentors at Harvard, John Mason Brown, the theatre critic, and Theodore Morrison encouraged the expectation that ultimately must be my destiny. Except that I had no idea as to how to become and to survive as a writer; nor had I anything in particular to write about. Instead, aroused by the challenge of economic crisis and the threat of war, I was drawn to the apparatus of government. Then the war itself, and the Navy. But the expectation, the idea of a literary career was not dead. And the primary objective of my 'retooling' under the GI Bill was to explore that possibility. The doctorate was to be a back up, an insurance against failure to make it as a novelist.

Robbins proposed some interesting dissertation topics with solid research opportunities, but the fieldwork that would be required for a solid research project was not what I had in mind. I wanted to stay at my desk and whip a thesis off the top of my head with time to work on my novel. So when Robbins suggested as a topic 'the presuppositions of economic theory' I jumped to accept. I thought I could spin it from the whole cloth. And a very bad choice it was, as Nicholas Kaldor, Hungarian and Buddha-like, forewarned me.

Because of the philosophical character of the topic, a new member of the LSE faculty was brought in to supervise my dissertation jointly with Robbins. This was Karl Popper, now Sir Karl 'Popper, who one day would be widely acknowledged as the world's foremost philosopher of science.

KARL POPPER

Popper had arrived in England from New Zealand to take a post as reader at the LSE in early January 1946, at about the same time as I did. I was probably his first graduate student. He was then 44 years old. I was 14 years his junior.

Popper was short, stocky like myself, very energetic, keen witted and intense. We communicated easily. Our argument was a pleasure. I liked him very much.

Born in Vienna, both his parents were baptized Jews. His father, an admirable man, a lawyer by profession, an historian by vocation, who played a role in relieving the desperate plight of the Austrian working class, was financially destroyed by the inflation in the aftermath of the First World War. Karl was 'formed' in the materially impoverished but incredibly rich cultural life of the Viennese intellectual. He worked as a manual labourer, as a cabinet maker, as a social worker with neglected children, as an elementary school teacher, as a high school teacher. He took successive doctorates in the history of music, in psychology, finally in philosophy where he found his niche. His *Logik der Forschung* (Julius Springer Verlag, 1935),[1] was well received. Because of it he was invited to lecture in various European countries. In 1935 he came to deliver a series of lectures in Great Britain; but also to look for an escape from the dangers for the Jew and the intellectual that he foresaw in the Hitlerian maelstrom. He gave a number of lectures in England on problems of physics, mathematics and philosophy; and also, at Professor Hayek's seminar at LSE, with Lionel Robbins also in attendance, he read an anti-Marxist tract titled 'The Poverty of Historicism'. While in England he answered an advertisement for, and subsequently was offered a readership in philosophy at Canterbury University College, Christchurch, New Zealand.

From 1937 until 1945, he and his wife lived and worked in New Zealand where, further developing 'The Poverty of Historicism', he wrote, and after great difficulty but with Hayek's help, in 1945 published *The Open Society and its Enemies* (George Routledge and Sons, London). That same year he accepted a readership that Hayek offered him at the London School of Economics.

Philosophy and the philosophy of science were no part of its normal curriculum, and Popper was not brought into the London School of Economics and Political Science to teach philosophy or to philosophize about science. Robbins and Hayek knew him only as an anti-communist, anti-socialist, anti-Marxist crusader. It was as such, with the publication of *The Open Society and its Enemies* that he first gained an international reputation.

as Isaiah Berlin writes in his biography of Karl Marx, Popper's *The Open Society and its Enemies* contains 'the most scrupulous and formidable criticism of the philosophical and historical doctrines of Marxism by any living writer'.

Brian Magee, *Karl Popper*
(The Viking Press, New York, 1973 p. 2.)

Or so I would reconstruct the scenario.

The London School of Economics was founded by Fabian socialists like George Bernard Shaw and Sidney and Beatrice Webb in order to provide a strong intellectual base for British socialism. During my undergraduate days at Harvard it was known as a centre of leftist, socialist thought. I even remember an incident in London in 1947 when I was taken aside by an American in striped pants (presumably from the State Department) to warn me that the LSE was a den of commies (or some equivalent). Whatever had once been the case, with the postwar victory of the Labour Party, the left-wing stars of the School migrated into the British govern-ment from the Prime Ministership down, leaving the field clear for Lionel Robbins. Robbins was an ideological liberal and a man of the Establishment. In the United States he would have belonged to the Chicago School. His outlook would know its glory days under Margaret Thatcher and Ronald Reagan. To strengthen his ideological regime, and with his indubitable eye for quality, he brought in Hayek as his right-hand and Popper as his left, the latter perhaps seen as offsetting the force of Harold Laski a brilliant leftist who was still a notable at the school.

Popper's logic or psychology of discovery supposes a primal need among mankind to achieve the settled, the regular, the certain. The search for, the achievement of, and the commitment to the settled, the regular, the certain, constitutes the dogmatic phase of thought. This phase is not only the opposite of, but is also the prerequisite for and prelude to a critical phase of question and challenge, of opposition and discovery. It is the dogmatic that provides the framework and stepping-stone for its opposite in the positive advance of knowledge. He thus proposes the logic or psychology of scientific advance as a process, not unlike the Hegelian dialectic, with the dogmatic playing the role of thesis, and the critical of the antithesis. Consider, for example, Popper's argument concerning the development of polyphony.

Given the heritage of the Greeks, and the development (and canonization) of the Church modes in the time of Ambrose and Gregory the Great, there would hardly have been any need for, or any incitement to, the invention of polyphony if Church musicians had the same freedom as, let us say, the originators of folk song. My conjecture was that it was the canonization of Church melodies, the *dogmatic restriction* on them, which produced the *cantus firmus* against which the counterpoint could develop. It was the established *cantus firmus* which provided the framework, the order, the regularity that made possible inventive freedom without chaos.

Karl Popper, *Unended Quest: An Intellectual Autobiography.* Revised edition (Open Court Publishing Company, La Salle and London, 1982) p. 58.

Whatever the general truth of this proposition, it very well applies to the development of Popper's own social and political thinking. He began as a communist and then became a social democrat. The commitment to Marxism was his dogmatic phase; the rejection of Marxism, his critical phase. Marxism was the *'cantus firmus'* framework for the inventive development of his social and political ideas.

The incident that led to his rejection of Marxism throws light on his character.

The incident that turned me against communism, and that soon led me away from Marxism altogether, was one of the most important incidents in my life. It happened shortly before my seventeenth birthday. In Vienna, shooting broke out during the demonstrations by un-armed young socialists who, instigated by the commun-ists, tried to help some communists to escape who were under arrest at the central police station in Vienna. Several young socialist and communist workers were killed. I was horrified and shocked by the brutality of the police, but also by myself. For I felt that as a Marxist I bore part of the responsibility for the tragedy – at least in principle. Marxist theory demands that the class struggle be intensified, in order to speed up the coming of socialism. Its thesis is that although the revolution may claim some victims, capitalism is claiming more victims than the whole socialist revolution.

That was the Marxist theory – part of the so-called 'scientific socialism.' I now asked myself whether such a calculation could ever be supported by 'science.' The whole experience, and especially this question, produced in me a life-long revulsion of feeling.

I realized the dogmatic character of the creed, and its incredible intellectual arrogance. It was a terrible thing to arrogate to oneself a kind of knowledge which made it a duty to risk the lives of other people for an uncritically accepted dogma or for a dream that might not turn out to be realizable. It was particularly bad for an intellectual, for one who could read and think. It was awfully depressing to have fallen into such a trap.

Ibid., pp. 33–4.

Aside from any question as to the correctness or incorrectness of Marxist theory, or as to the advisability of change through violent revolution, how are we to understand the reaction of Popper, a young communist, to this particular incident which itself in no way contradicted but in the strongest sense confirmed Marxist doctrine?

A young communist witnesses the brutal attack by the police on his unarmed and peacefully demonstrating friends and companions. Some are shot to death. What will be his response? If he is upright and courageous, that incident of itself would wed him more closely than before to the struggle against the state and system that perpetuated the brutality and injustice he had witnessed, and to the doctrine that precisely forewarned of brutal repression. But if he is not quite so upright and courageous? If he is timid and fearful of authority? Then, terrorized by the translation of theory into action, of words into hurt, pain and death, he might (as I might have, and I conjecture as Karl Popper did) surrender, submit and withdraw from the struggle as too dangerous for his taste.

With that withdrawal comes guilt and shame at having abandoned his beliefs and at having broken solidarity with his fallen comrades at the first sight of danger. To escape his guilt, to protect his self-esteem he denies that which he has betrayed. On what grounds? Because it was not 'scientific' inasmuch as the doctrine did not assure certainty in the final outcome; that in a world where there are no certain outcomes. His 'life-long revulsion', was aroused not against the state and system that had perpetrated the brutality and injustice he had witnessed but against 'Marxist theory — part of so-called 'scientific socialism'. Anti-Marxism becomes his shield against guilt, an assertion that what he done was not a shameful act but a worthy, even an heroic one.

My personal experience also would support the supposition that for all his boldness in argument, Karl Popper was timid, submissive and accommodating to the word of established authority.

In supervising my dissertation, Karl Popper introduced me to the philosophy of science. In the chapters that follow I will first consider the theory and problems of, and the rules laid down by, the philosophy of science; and then that which is implied by the application of these rules and theories to economics. My focus on economics is less parochial than might at first appear since economics is considered the most 'advanced' of the social sciences and serves as a model for the others. Since economics and the other social sciences share the same reference universe, hence the arguments to be made here will be relevant for all the social sciences.

SCIENCE AS THE CRITERION OF TRUTH

The philosophy of science is not about the philosophies of scientists, nor does it speculate philosophically about science qua phenomenon. It is about that which is required to approach true knowledge. Its linkage to science is in the idea that science, and particularly Newtonian physics, provides the model wherewith to differentiate the meaningful from the meaningless, sense from nonsense, science from non-science. Following this model the philosophy of science deduced the rule that scientific truth must be verified through precise and accurate prediction.

It was Popper's particular contribution to assert that prediction cannot prove that a statement is true but only that a statement is false; that such falsification through the test of prediction clears away falsehoods and opens the path towards an ever elusive truth. Hence that the heart of science is the constant exposure of its tentatively accepted laws, theories and hypotheses to tests of derivative predictions (If A is true then it can be logically deduced that B must follow. Does it?)

Popper was unequivocally committed to this criterion of falsification as demarcating science from non-science and marking out the path to true knowledge. His criterion required that every scientific theory, hypothesis, proposition, statement be so formulated that it can be tested through inferential prediction; and if it failed to meet any authentic test of derivative prediction, that it be discarded as false.

For Popper this was not only an ideal to be aspired to. He affirmed also that it approximated the actual practice that carried science forward. It was moreover the criterion to be used in establishing the credibility of statement in the social as well as the physical sciences.

APPLYING POPPER'S RULE

I learned from Popper that the method of science requires that statements put forward as laws, theories, hypotheses must be put to tests of derivative prediction, and that those that fail the test of any specific prediction are thereby falsified and ready for discard. Hence that any discipline whose statements cannot be so falsified is *ipso facto* not a science. It was on that ground that Popper attacked Marxist economics, relegating it to the limbo of pseudo-science.

I set about my study of the 'presuppositions of economic theory' selecting for an in-depth analysis four major and representative works of Western (Neo-Classical and Keynesian) economics: Marshall's *Principles*, Pigou's *Welfare Economics*, Keynes's *General Theory*, and Hicks's *Value and Capital*.

At the time I did not doubt Popper's authority. I accepted his criterion of falsification. I accepted his demarcation of science and non-science. I accepted his argument that the function of testing through specific derivative prediction was to separate out the host of falsehood and superstition from the domain of the possibly true. I was ready to apply, indeed I had no honest option but to apply the criterion I had learned from him as the proper rule in the demarcation of non-science and in the identification of falsehood, to the allegedly great works of Marshall, Pigou, Keynes and Hicks. As he had critiqued Marxist economics, it was my task to critique Keynesian and Neo-Classical economics. And there was the rub.

I realized, I could not help but quickly realizing that under Popper's rule, these great works of Keynesian and Neo-Classical economics were not science. Their large general statements, their theories had never survived, indeed had never been made subject to the test of falsification through derivative prediction. Put forward as 'tendencies', 'trends', 'propensities', they were not falsifiable by any specific test of derivative prediction. If they had been stated in a falsifiable form, one saw that they would at once be falsified by a myriad of specifically predictable events. And in a rare instance, like that of Malthusian theory where prediction was clear and unequivocal, a century and a half of failed prediction did not affect their status. According to Popper's rule, Western economics was a non-science, a pseudo-science; and Popper's critique of Marxism applied with equal or greater force to Western economics.

But I did not condemn Western economics on that account, nor suppose it to be a case of retarded development that would right itself in time as the discipline advanced. I held that Popper's rule could never apply to social science because of the nature of the universe to which the general statements of economics or of any of the social sciences, must refer. And I worked to develop a philosophy and criteria, and rules of credibility, appropriate to generalizing statement in the social sciences. All this will be developed in the chapters that follow.

DOOMED

Thus my dilemma.

The economics practised by Robbins and his cohorts was outside the boundaries of scientific inquiry as those boundaries had been drawn by Popper. That was one inescapable fact.

Robbins, best known for his book *An Essay on the Nature and Significance of Economic Science* (Macmillan, London, 1935)[2], forewarned me by indirection of the pit that lay ahead. That he, Archbishop of the Faith, merciless of heresy, would reject and abjure the attack I was destined to make in denying the 'scientific' legitimacy of the doctrine and dogma over which he presided, was the other inescapable fact. Between the devil and the deep blue sea. My goose was cooked and I knew it.

I called the doomed dissertation *Essence, Evaluation and Social Technology*. Make no mistake, I did my best to appease the powers that held my fate in their hands. I did not propose the discard of economic theory because it failed the test of falsification. I tried otherwise to rationalize its retention. I did my best to divert attention from my fatal conclusions. I covered them over with a thicket of other theories and arguments. I even designed and proposed a whole reconstruction of economics and a reorganization of the entire social inquiry: in more than seven hundred pages. I would have welcomed being shown the error of my ways. I would have been happy to answer objections, to make corrections, in any way to accommodate. I waited in numbed anticipation for the rituals of judgment to commence, and for my sentence to be pronounced.

Never once during the long passage of time towards the inevitable denouement was anything in the dissertation ever questioned or criticized. No one ever objected to, criticized or questioned the substance of my argument, not even in the charade of an oral defence. Robbins who would normally serve as the internal examiner, had broken off contact and divorced himself from the proceedings. In his place was an unknown, whom I had never seen or heard of before, who, instructed, remained totally silent throughout. The external examiner was the dour Roy Harrod from Cambridge, who questioned me only on obscure points of Keynes's *General Theory*, entirely unrelated to my arguments. I made no protest. Like a bird trapped in the eye of a snake, I was paralysed into submission by the foreknowledge of my fate. Anathema had been whispered and there was no recourse.

When it was over Karl Popper came to visit me at my home, to confide that mine had ideas sufficient for eighty dissertations, urging me to continue with it, recalling the many times he had rewritten *The Open Society*. I had no indication that he ever actively expressed himself in my defence. Who could blame him, the refugee newcomer to

England, for deferring to his powerful patron? In any case it would have been useless.

Though for a generation Popper would serve as reader and professor at this school for the social sciences, he seems never to have published anything about the 'science' of economics or about social science. Would he have learned from my experience those many years ago not to incur the displeasure of his patrons by exposing the non-science in the 'sciences' they practiced?

Harold Laski came to read the dissertation after I had left England. He complained that I had whored after side issues; but he sent me word via his student Joseph Goldstein who has become a professor of law at Yale, that if I returned to the LSE he would grant me a doctorate on the basis of it. But by then for me there could be no turning back.

This nevertheless was a first phase in my coming to conceptualize and comprehend the phenomenon of science, in this instance at the level of epistemology, considering the criterion of scientific knowledge applied to (and tested against) the realities of economics and, inferentially, of the other social sciences.

The epistemological is but one aspect of the idea of science. There are others. In what follows, with apologies to those to whom apologies may be due, I will try to explain how I came to encounter and comprehend some of these other facets of science, so that they became a part of my professional equipage: facets that will be brought into play later in the development of my argument.

COOPERATIVE RESEARCH ASSOCIATIONS IN THE UNITED KINGDOM

At the end of the First World War, cognizant of the Germany's successful application of science to the needs of industry, the British government established cooperative research associations to service the needs of each British industry. These were supported first by contributions from the government and from the beneficiary firms in the industry; and later by dues exclusively from the beneficiary firms. At the time I was in England, an ex-refugee business-man made a grant to LSE to study the experience of those cooperative research associations.

The grant was given and the study undertaken by Ronald Edwards on the faculty at LSE who was my wife's super-visor and who hired her as his assistant. It was their intention that she should do her dissertation on that subject.

Ronald Edwards was an accountant, the prototype accountant out of a story by Dickens: his gaunt form draped in dark serge, his beady eyes enlarged behind thick lens, his red raw-looking skin drawn tight over a face like a clenched fist, all bones and angles perched on a scrawny neck rising from the centre of the round collar, with his sharp-pointed Adams apple bobbing. He too was a protégé of Robbins. I think of him as standing stiff behind his relaxed and genial master as the tight-fisted bailiff on the feudal estate who would hold the tenants to account for every stolen apple. Was it that traditional system of control by the aristocrat and bailiff that explains the extraordinarily important role of the accountant in British affairs?

Two years into my studies at LSE, my dissertation doomed but not yet rejected, a time of hiatus while I waited for the axe to fall; working intermittently, trying in vain to squeeze out inspiration for the novel; taking care of our house and of our baby girl; allowing my wife to spend all her time at the School presumably to work on her dissertation, I was ready for something, anything to fill those desperate hours.

Edwards, it appeared, was not satisfied with the draft chapters submitted by my wife. He suggested that she ask me to rework the 'style' of those chapters. I had a reputation on that score at the School, gained perhaps through Robbins and a paper I had given at the faculty seminar. This suggestion surprised me, but I took her material all the same and started working it over. In the uneasy emptiness of my days I drew the subject matter of her dissertation hungrily into the vacuum of my thought. I reworked the material to give it clarity and coherence; and deduced what implications I could for policy and practice.

RESEARCH AND DEVELOPMENT; SCIENCE AS AN ELEMENT OF THE DYNAMIC ECONOMY

In the course of doing this I experienced one of those curious realizations wherein the curtain is suddenly raised to reveal the deeper significance of commonplace knowledge and ordinary experience. I understood that via the phenomenon of research and development (R&D), science had come into the market place, that it was or could become crucial as motor force in the dynamic of the modern industrial economy; a realization that was then quite outside the scope of academic awareness. There was no place for it in the economist's mode of thinking. It fitted none of the prevailing theories. No one of the established schools of economic thought had taken it into account. It was moreover a science of a different sort than that envisaged by Karl Popper and other philosophers of science. This was no autonomous discourse of free individuals in the disinterested pursuit of truth. It was systematically-organized, directed, technologically-oriented, harnessed to the goals of industry, of medicine, and of military power.

Neither Neo-Classical nor Keynesian economics could explain technological change, or innovation, or the process of technological advance. For Neo-Classical economics, rising productivity was no more than a function of capital accumulation. In the annals of economic thought, only the late, great Joseph Schumpeter, who had been my teacher at Harvard, had developed a theory to explain technological advance in the capitalist economy. His *The Theory of*

Capitalist Development (Cambridge, Mass., Harvard University Press, 1934) focussed on technological innovation and its
consequences for employment and investment. In his
system, the introduction of new technology was an
extraordinary event brought about through the action of
an heroic individual (the innovator) who acted in defiance of
the rational entrepreneurial calculus, to swim against the
tides of expectations and the resistance of ingrained practice
and of vested interests. But such innovation assumed the
prior existence of that which was to be innovated. From
whence came the new technology that the innovator
introduced? Schumpeter took the invention, the genesis
and development of the new technologies, as something
given, as in the air so to speak, waiting to be seized upon by
the bold and resourceful innovator. I contrasted the
Schumpetarian model with the regime of R&D where the
genesis, development and introduction of new technology
was organized as an integral system and integrated into the
normal competitive practices of the market.[3] All of this,
which was quite aside from the discussion of the cooperative
research associations, I wrote into my soon-to-be ex-wife's
dissertation.

Through this chance encounter I came to see in science
two distinct and fundamentally different forms of organization, with R&D harnessed to the goals of society and
providing a crucial element in the dynamics of modern
industry.

SCIENCE POLICY, AND THE ECONOMICS OF R&D

In 1949 I returned to the United States without the
doctorate, without my marriage, without my child, without
the prospect of a job in McCarthy-ridden Washington. I
worked for a year writing scripts for television, then
enrolled at Cornell University seeking again to obtain the
doctorate. When the time came to select a dissertation topic,

I steered clear of the philosophy of science but pursued my interest in research and development.

The prime *technological* choice of the American government during and after the Second World War was in confronting the closure of American imports of natural rubber from Malaysia as a consequence of the lightning-like Japanese conquest of the region. This involved the American government's decision to establish under public aegis a new industry to produce rubber synthetically; and after the war the need to so develop the technology that the new industry would be commercially viable. That was the subject of my dissertation.

It was at once a study of complex decision-taking on issues of science and technology in the American political context, and of the rationale of public and corporate choice in the organization and direction of research and development under the circumstances of war and peace. It led to the first serious publications at least in the United States on the formation of science policy, and on the economics of research and development.[4]

Thus a third milestone in my personal discovery of the facets of science: from its role in epistemology, to its dynamic function in the market economy; to the economics of R&D, and the formation of science policy.

SOCIAL SYSTEMS AND ECONOMIC ORGANIZATIONS

I did not become a specialist. I taught in university after university, and moved from academia into consulting and from consulting back to the academy; and my interests wandered far and wide over the terrain of thought. But, perhaps because I was sensitized to seek it, I encountered, observed, studied and wrote about divers facets of science at various points in my new career[5]: for example as a consultant to the Economic Development Administration in Puerto Rico where I had a hand in establishing the petro-chemical complex there,[6] or as project director for the National Planning Association where I studied and wrote about the alleged spillover of benefits from space-military R&D into the civilian industrial economy[7], or as consultant to the Science Directorate of the Organization for Economic Cooperation and Development (OECD) in Paris where, for example, I did a comparative study of the mobilization of scientific resources for technical assistance to less developed countries,[18] or as consultant to Jim Webb, Administrator of NASA in its glory days.[9]

The consequence of all this? I came to understand science as a set of systems and as a component of systems, interacting with other elements in some functional performance.

Systems?

One specializes, to become expert (say) concerning the parts of the human body: the tissues, or the skeletal structure, or the blood, or the organs, or the brain, the nerves; or more specifically of the heart, of the arteries, of the lungs, of the teeth and the tongue, of the nose and the throat, of the eyes, of the ears, of the spine and the hip and the knees, of the stomach and the colon, of the liver and the kidneys, of the feet, of the genitals, of the skin. These, though studied and understood as individual components of the body, find their significance in interacting together and interacting with elements outside the body, as coherent systems of, say, locomotion, reproduction, digestion, respiration, growth. The components of the body and the elements of the environment that will be brought within the boundaries of a system, depends on the operation to be described, or on the problem to be solved, or on the question that is asked.

So also components of a society and elements external to society combine as systems for the performance of social functions; nor will their functional performance be comprehended except by reference to a systemic interaction.

Popper thought of science as a system of thought; which it is, though by no means the only system of thought. Nor is it only a system of thought. It is also a system for the communication and of dissemination of information. It is also a system of recruitment and training, of incentives and supports. It is a system for the selection of problems, i.e., a system of choice and of power. Where the systems of culture (of values and evaluation) and of politics (power) intersect, science splits into sub-systems depending upon whether choice is made by reference to market values, military values, or academic values. Science may be among the components of a system of technological advance, or of a system of learning, or of a system of economic development.

The idea of science as a functional system in a world of systems was a final milestone on my path of discovery.[10]

2

Popper's Progress

THE POSITIVIST CURRENT OF THOUGHT

Our emphasis has been on Karl Popper as representing a current of thought with deep roots in history; a current of thought that we will call *positivist*. It reflects the belief in a process of cumulative learning through experience that has drawn mankind out of dark and ancient depths towards the single lodestone of truth. It projects an image of history as the slow but certain triumph of a reason that, through the trials of experience, learns to differentiate the true from the false, piercing the clouds of obscurantism and superstition, turning the vast spaces of ignorance into light.[1]

It conceives of man as a creature of reason and of society as evolving through the force of reason; where the essence of being is reason realizing itself, of reason clearing its space in the primal darkness, of reason incrementally, cumulatively, exposing the infinite depths and complexity of objective reality to the light of understanding.

It is an outlook that came to embody the faith in progress and the optimism of the nineteenth century, finding in the history of society an analogue to the Darwinian evolution of the species. Like all the species, social man is endowed with the will to survive but also with the drive to comprehend, to understand, to seek for truth. Through that drive, mutations are generated in the corpus of knowledge. These too must meet the test of experience so that man's knowledge is itself the product of an evolutionary process. It is a process, however, given the social capacity to communicate, to record and accumulate, and to disseminate the stuff of knowledge, that is infinitely more rapid than its Darwinian counterpart.

21

In all this, the apotheosis was science. Science, in positivist thought, is the ultimate mutation of that evolutionary process, the ideal instrument of reason in the pursuit of true knowledge, and a model for every disciplined effort to understand reality. The speculations of traditional epistemology are replaced by a philosophy of science where:

> transcendental inquiry into the conditions of possible knowledge can be meaningfully pursued only in form of methodological inquiry into the rules for the construction and corroboration of scientific theories . . . Positivism marks the end of the theory of knowledge. In its place emerges the philosophy of science. Transcendental logical inquiry into the conditions of possible knowledge aimed as well at explicating the meaning of knowledge as such. Positivism cuts off this inquiry, which it conceives as having become meaningless in virtue of the fact of modern science.
>
> Jürgen Habermas, *Knowledge and Human Interest*
> (Boston, Beacon Press, 1972), p. 67.

The philosopher's favoured model of science was of classical mechanics:

(1)   where all changes are reversible,
(2)   where all outcomes are predetermined and conceivably predictable,
(3)   hence where an appropriate means of testing the truth of statement is through the precise prediction of specific outcomes,
(4)   and where time is without substantive content but only constitutes a space for the unfolding of predetermined relationships.

From this model the philosophers deduced universal rules to be applied in the pursuit of authentic truth about physical, biological, psychological and social realities.

The domain of man and society is equated to that of classical mechanics. Thus D. M. Armstrong gives a positivist answer to the questions. ' Is man nothing more than a physical body? Can we give a complete account of man in purely physical terms?'

It seems increasingly likely that biology is completely reducible to chemistry which is, in its turn, completely reducible to physics. This is to say, it seems increasingly likely that all chemical and biological happenings are explicable in principle as particular applications of the laws of physics that govern non-chemical and non-biological phenomena. [p. 49]

. . . it seems very unlikely that psychology is an exception. [p. 503]

D. M. Armstrong, *A Materialist Theory of the Mind* (London and New York, Routledge & Kegan Paul, 1968).

What does modern science have to say about the nature of man? There are, of course, all sorts of disagreements and divergencies in the views of individual scientists. But I think it fair to say that one view is steadily gaining ground, so that it bids fair to become an established scientific doctrine. This is the view that we can give a complete account of man in *purely physico-chemical terms*. This view has received a tremendous impetus in recent decades from the new subject of molecular biology, a subject that promises to unravel the physical and chemical mechanisms that lie at the basis of life. Before that time it received great encouragement from pioneering work in neurophysiology pointing to the likelihood of a purely electro-chemical account of the working of the brain. [p. 1]

D. M. Armstrong, *The Nature of the Mind* (Ithaca, Cornell University Press, 1980).

Certainly there are significant differences between (in our sense) positivist philosophers, like Pierce and James, the early Wittgenstein and Russell, the logical positivists of the Vienna Circle and Karl Popper. Popper's contribution to this positivist stream of thought has been particularly:

(1)   in formulating the criterion for differentiating science from non-science, and truth from falsehood,
(2)   in forwarding an idea of the actual, historical operation of science in the pursuit of knowledge.

His central contribution was simple and decisive. It was to assert that successful prediction is no criterion of truth. No amount of successful prediction can ever establish the truth of a statement in science. The function of prediction is not to verify but to refute, not to establish truth but to eliminate falsehoods. The unequivocal failure of a single, specific, prediction accurately deduced from a given hypothesis, theory, or proposition would serve to falsify and ready for discard that hypothesis, theory or proposition.

His criterion throughout is the rule of falsification. Under his rule all statements about reality are considered as never more than conjectural. Since no amount of verification can prove the truth of a statement, science can only, through the test of derivative prediction, prove a statement to be false; and through a continuum of such testing, science weeds out error and falsehood. The credibility of statement in science requires that such statement has been continuously tested and has not yet failed the test of precise and specific prediction. It is this capacity for precise, specific prediction and its exercise, that differentiates science from non-science.

Like the whole of modern positivist thought, Popper's argument derives its force from the alleged success of the physical sciences. BE LIKE PHYSICS is the rule behind all the rules. Hence an idea is innate as to what physics, in actual practice, is, and how it works as a social organization and an historical phenomenon. Popper's theory supposes that each science operates continuously to extend the logical and predictive reach of every established theory in order to account for what was hitherto inexplicable. Striving to extend, and in extending further testing its predictive powers, each theory eventually encounters its limits, and fails the test of derivative prediction. By that failure, it is proven false and made ready for discard. Its falsification spurs the development of new and competitive theories that would encompass and transcend the explanatory power of the old. The new theory in turn reaches out to extend the scope of understanding, until, submitted to the tests of derivative prediction, it too reaches its limits, fails the test and is falsified. On and on. We will refer to Popper's thesis and its context as 'the canon'.

One might reasonably claim that in the 1930s and 1940s with Popper's *Logic of Discovery*, this positivist stream of thought reached its culmination. With Popper, the positivist idea of science reached not only its pre-eminence but also its limit. For these developments threatened its very foundations.

DOUBT

The optimism of the nineteenth century, its faith in progress and in reason as the innate and irrepressible force of history, its belief in science as the benefactor, even saviour of mankind, unfailing as a criterion of truth, are profoundly in disaccord with the experiences of the twentieth century.

It has been a time of genocide, politicide, terror, violence, persecutions without end. Two wars have drenched the world in blood, with the prospect of a third that will destroy the species. It has known an economic collapse where for a decade, people starved while the means of production rusted in idleness. It saw the rise of Fascism, and the incredible moral retrogression of Germany under Hitler where the

Nazis came within a hair's breadth of world conquest and the destruction of civilization. It saw the golden dream of socialism destroyed to the muted cries and screams of the slain and tortured millions in Stalin's Russia, and in Mao's China. It witnessed the Holocaust. In producing the bomb, science prepared our common pyre. A science-based technology, omnivorous of irreplaceable resources, has polluted the sea and the air, pushing us to the edge of a precipice. Progress is no longer self-evidently the innate quality of historical time. Shrieks and curses drown the voice of reason. Science sometimes appears as a blind monster to be feared, watched, monitored.

THE CANON NEEDS A DETERMINANT WORLD

Whether the canon is applied to the physical or the social sciences, the canon requires a determinant world where all events in a closed system are predetermined with absolute precision. For this simple reason. If X causes A today and causes B tomorrow, and maybe C thereafter — then no specific derivative prediction can falsify the theory of X.

This posed no problem for the application of the canon under the regime of Newtonian physics. But with twentieth-century quantum mechanics and thermodynamics, physics became indeterminant and an indeterminance seemed to have asserted itself at the heart of the physical world.

THE CHALLENGE OF QUANTUM MECHANICS

Quantum mechanics, developed by Werner Heisenberg in 1925, threw physics into a state of division and turmoil that lasted well beyond the Second World War. Popper on the periphery of the world of professional physicists, who had started to write his *Logik* in 1930, was caught up in this 'dissension and confusion'. He writes:

> These all too superficial remarks will perhaps explain why I felt at a loss when I first tried to come to grips with quantum mechanics . . . I was working on my own from books and from articles; the only physicist with whom I sometimes talked about my difficulties was my friend Franz Urbach. I tried to understand the theory and he had doubts whether it was understandable — at least by ordinary mortals.
>
> Popper, *Unended Quest*, p. 91.

Popper wrestled hard and long to overthrow or subdue the demon of indeterminance, but the tides of time were overwhelming. In 1949 he is still far from surrendering. He describes his position:

> There is no such thing as a specifically quantum-mechanical argument against determinism. Of course quantum mechanics is a statistical theory and not a prima facie determinist one, but that does not mean it is incompatible with a prima facie determinist theory. (More specifically Von Neumann's famous proof of this alleged incompatibility . . . is invalid.) The position that I had arrived at in 1934 was that nothing in quantum mechanics justifies the thesis that determinism is refuted because of its incompatibility with quantum mechanics. Since then I have changed my mind on this issue more than once.
>
> Ibid., p. 94.

But in 1949 we find Popper delivering the William James Lecture at Harvard University, meeting with Einstein at Princeton and urging the great man to accept an indeterminant physical world.

What then of falsification?

PROBABILITY

Popper put his trust in probability, in the expectation that where one could not predict a specific outcome, one could predict a specific random distribution, and on that basis, falsify. He laboured to find a formula that would thus protect the falsification criterion.

Though it serves the practical needs of the working scientist, probability provides no safe haven for the canon. Given an open-ended series of events, there can be no certain distribution of event. Arbitrary limits must, as a matter of judgment, be imposed to set the boundaries of the sample considered credible; and that selection reflects a judgment of the evidence pro and con; a judgment that is as much one of verification as of falsification. Jacob Bronowski explains:

[Probability] has rightly preoccupied Popper . . . His main views seem to me clear, steadfast and wholly right. Probability in this view is a concrete property of physical systems in which the events overall come out in a consistent way but not in a unique way. In such systems, probability is an inferred or theoretical entity which we do not observe directly, much as an electron is — and it is real in the same sense. I share this view of probability, and so I think do most physicists now; though I prefer to express it by saying that probability can only be ascribed to events that have a *distribution*, and must be read as a symbol for the distribution as a whole . . . . the status or plausibility of a scientific theory cannot be described by a probability, because there is no unique distribution in which it has its place. Of course, the status of a theory goes up or down with the evidence for it; but this is not the same as having an assignable probability.

My purpose is to examine Popper's use of probability at two crucial places: in the testing of theories which predict events that are only probable, and in the formation and assessment of theories of any kind.

When a theory predicts several possible outcomes for an experiment, it is hard to tell what set of outcomes is different enough from a predicted set to falsify the theory. Strictly speaking, we should no doubt say that it is impossible to tell. The predicted outcomes of a string of experiments are all the possible samples of that size from the postulated distribution: and whatever the actual outcomes are, they certainly form a possible sample. Of course the samples of a given size from the postulated distribution have a known distribution in their turn, and we can calculate how improbable it is that we should have drawn our actual sample by bad luck alone. But this regress does not help us make an absolute decision that the theory is false, yes or no, however far we continue it. The sample we have drawn may be wildly improbable, but it is not impossible. How long ought we watch a tossed penny come down heads before we can be sure that we are being cheated — the penny is bad? Strictly speaking, for ever.

The Logic of Scientific Discovery met this difficulty . . . by fixing an arbitrary limit to the process of decision. In effect, Popper proposed that, if the collective outcome of a string of outcomes is too improbable, we treat that as equivalent to falsification. . . . That is a sensible way to interpret experiments in practice, and it is in fact the way scientists use. But in principle it removes the test of falsification from the singular eminence to which Popper had raised it. In the first place, it makes the test arbitrary, by leaving us to fix the range of improbability that is to be accepted as zero. In the second place it suffers from the usual regress implicit in such ranges (and in all measures of the probability of a probability), because the end points of the range have to be surrounded in turn by their own ranges, and so on. And in the third and chief place, it invites the same privilege for the test of verification that we have just allowed for the test of falsification. We can hardly make a scheme of approximate falsification, and elevate it (in effect) to a sufficient falsification without granting the same liberty to verification. Of course verification is only provisional, but the point is that in this scheme, falsification is also only provisional . . .

A theory that makes only probable predictions cannot be strictly falsified by any run of its alternative outcomes. For such theories (that is for most modern theories) the test by falsification is no more decisive than the test by verification. Popper rightly criticized verification because it must be inconclusive: but in the fundamental theories of modern science falsification can do no better — and no worse. Both offer evidence for or against a theory and no more.

Paul Arthur Schlipp (ed.), *The Philosophy of Karl Popper*,
pp. 615–16.

FREEDOM

In delivering the Arthur Holly Compton Memorial Lecture in 1965 Popper came the full circle. Now he welcomed and joined with Compton in hailing quantum mechanics for having introduced physical indeterminance and thereby freeing mankind from the 'nightmare of the physical determinist' wherein 'because the laws of physics were assumed correct' therefore:

all our thoughts, feelings and efforts can have no practical influence upon what happens in the physical world; they are, if not mere illusions, at best superfluous by-products (epiphenomena) of physical events. . . . But, with the uncertainty, the indeterminance of quantum mechanics, . . . it is no longer justifiable to use physical law as evidence against human freedom.

POPPER'S RESPONSE TO THE CHALLENGE OF QUANTUM MECHANICS

Thus step by step Popper has retreated from a determined world. Step by step he accommodated to the indeterminance introduced by quantum mechanics, and in the end proclaimed it as the prerequisite and proof of human freedom. Step by step he abandoned the imperatives of the canon. Bronowski again:

Accordingly, Popper in his later work has more and more moved away from the sharp issues of scientific decision. He writes less about falsification and more about evidence: less about theories or hypotheses and more about problems: and he stresses the part played in science by argument and criticism. His picture of the scientist is no longer of the young man with an audacious theory, devising experiments that challenge nature to prove him wrong. Rather he is pictured now as a skeptical but benign Socratic elder (no doubt looking a little like an Austrian professor) discussing a problem with his staff, and unraveling it strand by strand until they are rationally persuaded to prefer his explanation to another. The critical steps in the discussion which lead them to reject another explanation still rely on experiments, of course,

but now the experimental results are accepted as convin-
cing without being decisive.

Schlipp, *The Philosophy of Karl Popper*, pp. 617–18.

Two important points:

(1)   Though Popper himself abandons the imperatives of
the canon, the canon remains unscathed. He has never
returned to repudiate, revise or replace it, for he has no
criterion of credibility to replace it with.

(2)   In a response that is characteristic and, in my view,
utterly bizarre, Popper and Compton both proclaim the
reality of human freedom, not because they have
looked upon themselves and their world and found it
so, but, because in quantum mechanics, freedom is
found to be not incompatible with physics.

THE PARADIGM AND THE EPISTIME

Popper's philosophy of science has been celebrated for its
focus on the working scientist and on science as a
functioning system. It deduces the falsibility rule from the
alleged practice of science, and justifies the rule by reference
to selected instances of its application. Hence the credibility
of Popper's philosophy depends not only on whether the
falsibility rule is applicable, workable and rational as a
recommended procedure, but also whether it accurately
describes the operation of science. Thomas Kuhn's, *The
Structures of Scientific Revolutions* (Chicago, University of
Chicago Press, 1962), deals a powerful blow against the
verity of the canon as an idea of the actual, historical
operation of science in the pursuit of knowledge.

Kuhn demonstrates that each of the sciences is bounded
and defined by a particular system of perception embodied
in a set of theories, hypotheses, techniques of inquiry and

analysis, model experiments, overt and covert assumptions, all deeply inculcated in the discipline and perpetuated through its successive generations. This system of perception Kuhn calls a paradigm.

'All scientists most of the time, most scientists all of the time' confine themselves to the elaboration of the paradigm. They select only problems susceptible to its analytic capabilities. They predict only that which is predictable within its frame, ignoring the predictive failures of established theories, shrugging off as anomalies observations that contradict its assumptions. Such is the 'normal' practice of science.

Each science exists as an island of the explicable within a sea of anomalies and contradictions. Occasionally, very rarely there occurs, for reasons Kuhn does not explain, a shattering transformation of the established paradigm. This Kuhn calls 'revolutionary science,' producing another paradigm. The new paradigm will in turn be as resistant to future contradictions of experience as the old one was.

Thus the reality of science is not of an unending series of falsification and discard. Though failures in prediction abound, the fundamental statement, the analytic framework, the apparatus of theory persists. No unilinear rise. No unambiguous drive in search of truth.

Michel Foucault whose work in France has only gradually and partially infiltrated Anglo-American awareness, departed even further than Kuhn from the positivist image of science. In his great work *The Order of Things* (New York, Random House, 1970), Foucault demonstrates that the revolutionary transformation of a particular paradigm of science does not occur in isolation. Such transformations take place in clusters. Within a period as short as two decades there are revolutionary transformations of science virtually across the board. And what is truly remarkable is that all these revolutionary transformations are at base the same transformation, reflecting the same change in an underlying mode of thought that Foucault calls the 'episteme'. Changes in this underlying mode of thought upon which the perceptions of the particular sciences depend, cannot be explained as a function of predictive failures or as a rational or even a conscious choice between alternatives.

With Kuhn and Foucault, the philosophy of science turns sharply away from the stream of positivist thought.

I have no reason to suppose that Popper knows of Foucault, but he is certainly familiar with Kuhn and the Kuhnsian critique. Part Two of the two volume, *The Philosophy of Karl Popper*, edited by Paul Arthur Schlipp is given as 'Descriptive and Critical Essays on the Philosophy of Karl Popper', and Part Three as 'The Philosopher Replies'. Here Kuhn contributes a critical essay and Popper replies to that critique.

Kuhn asserts fundamental differences between his views and Popper's, arguing that while Popper's logic of discovery might have value as ideal and as an apologia for science, it in no way explains or describes the sociological, the psychological, the operational realities of the science enterprise. Normal science, wherein the scientist engages in puzzle solving within a given analytic framework without challenging that framework, is the general, the usual, the nearly all-pervasive character of scientific activity. This does not mean that normal science is easy, trivial or routine. It can be brilliant and innovative like the chess of the master player, but like that of the chess master it operates within and makes no attempt to change the rules. Nor is it sterile. On the contrary it has been the source of vast advance in the accumulation of knowledge, e.g., in the development or discovery of new vaccines, surgical techniques, pharmaceuticals, galaxies, and elementary particles. Nor can these victories of normal science be accounted for in the dialectic of critical discourse. It is moreover only in normal science that there is a systematic testing of hypotheses through derivative prediction. Nor does revolutionary science follow Popper's rule as occurring though the correction of mistakes (was Ptolemaic astronomy a mistake?), where a falsified analytic system crumbles under the failed test of derivative prediction.

In his reply Popper concedes that he was never aware of 'normal science' until he read Kuhn's book. 'I closed my eyes to it because it was a kind of modern blemish in my essentially routine-free picture of science'[2] He considers normal science to be abnormal, an aberration, and a danger that could be 'the end of science as I see it.' Popper is quite right that since the end of the First World War with the advent of Research and Development, there has been a fundamental change in the organizational character of science, though he gives no evidence of having grasped the nature of that change. In his reply he reasserts his emphasis on critical thinking, but now with no word about falsification.

To understand Popper's full response to these institutional dimensions of science, and to indeterminance via quantum mechanics and thence the freedom of man, we return to the Holly Compton Memorial Lecture.

THREE WORLDS

That Popper (and Compton) accepted a margin of indeterminance in the physical world did not at all mean that they had come to accept society and the individual as something apart from the physical world and to consider human behaviour as no longer subordinated to and controlled by the laws of physics. The possibility of human freedom must be, for them, consistent with, even a function of quantum mechanics. But for physics, what remains in the absence of determinism is chance; and human behaviour as a function of chance left no place for planning, purpose, deliberation, creativity, nor any place for the critical discourse and the learning through the correction of error, so critical to Popper's philosophy. In the last part of the lecture, striving to reconcile the irreconcilable, Popper is clearly moving towards his conceptualization of the three worlds, which would come to play an important part in his thinking.

He conceives of three autonomous worlds. These are:

(1)   the physical world,
(2)   a world of mental states,
(3)   a world of objective knowledge including the things in which knowledge and information are embodied.

He proposes that human behaviour and social development can be explained in the interaction of these three. Thus he opens a place outside the sphere of the random for the creative-critical discourse in a purposeful and cumulative development of science.

AN APPROACHING SCIENTIFIC REVOLUTION

If the experience of the philosopher can be taken as a clue to developments in the broader stream of thought, then it would appear that the foundations of positivist thought are crumbling under the assault of the tragic irrationality and disappointments of our century, of an undetermined physical world and an indeterminant physics and the unresolved dilemmas of human freedom, and of a transformed understanding of the institutional and psychic understructure of scientific (and human) behaviour. The structure of positivist thought remains nevertheless, and the canon at its apex is unscathed; for there is as yet no criterion, no paradigm that can accommodate the forces of contradiction and challenge that erode and destroy its foundation. Is this then the formula? are these the signs of an approaching scientific revolution?

In the next chapter we will examine the inter-play between the philosophy of science and economics, as a prototype social science.

3

Popper's Canon, Kuhn's Paradigm and Economics

QUESTIONS

Chapter 2 described the character of positivist thought and its culmination in the canon. What has been the relationship of economics to positivist thought and the canon?

Chapter 2 also contrasted the views of Popper and Kuhn concerning the actualities of the science enterprise. How do these contrasting theories measure up against the practice of economics?

Chapter 2 analysed the rule of falsification *vis-à-vis* the advance of science. What role has falsification played in the development of economic thought?

Part 1 of this chapter will undertake to answer those questions.

In order to give depth to our arguments, Part 2 will review another critique of the canon in its role as a guide to economics. Part 3, in order to contrast nominal attitudes towards and actual practice concerning the imperatives of the canon, will review the famous controversy in economics as to whether or not a theory can be rejected because its assumptions are invalid.

1. THEORY AND PRACTICE

The Relationship of Economics to Positivist Thought

The methodology and outlook of Classical/Neo-Classical economics are integrally related to what we described as the stream of positivist thought. With its assumption of a universal rationality, no other discipline expresses the positivist outlook so well. Born of the same eighteenth century episteme as Classical physics, susceptible to the same intellectual imperatives, economics developed in a form that closely resembles the Newtonian model.[1] Keynes remarked of Alfred Marshall's theory of value:

> The general idea underlying the proposition that value is determined at the equilibrium point of demand and supply was extended to as to discover a whole Copernican system by which all elements of the economic universe are kept in their place by mutual counterpoise and interaction.[2]
>
> J. M. Keynes, *Essays in Biography* (London, Macmillan, 1933) p. 223.

Nor has economics ever ceased, like the modern philosophy of science, to look to physics as its criterion of science and as its methodological mentor.

There have been two major methodological innovations in economics during the twentieth century, namely the mathematization of its language, and its anathema on value judgment, the first associated with Paul Samuelson[3] and the second with Sir John Hicks.[4] Both Samuelson's *Foundations* and Hicks's *Value and Capital* were written in the late 1930s, long before Popper appeared on the scene. Samuelson explained the objective of his *Foundations* as to enable economics to verify and falsify its propositions through the test of precise and specific prediction. Thus the development of methodology in economics and the development of the modern philosophy of science have followed parallel paths. For both the rule behind the rules has been to BE LIKE PHYSICS.

Whether or not it has itself influenced the practice of economics, because it rationalizes the deep prior commitment of economics, the canon has been accepted by economists as the authoritative word.

BOUNDARIES

Popper sees the sciences as problem-oriented, where the problem comes first, with the discipline encompassing and the scientist taking into account whatever might be relevant to its solution. Kuhn sees the sciences as paradigm-based, with problems admissible into the discourse only if and inasmuch as they are solvable through an established analytic apparatus. Which of these two ideas of a science is true for economics?

Our focus is on Classical\Neo-Classical economics. Because it has dominated Western thought for more than two centuries, we will refer to it as establishment or mainstream economics. Its scope has been determined by the boundaries of a paradigm consisting of a particular core outlook, a distinctive set of theories, research techniques and model examples. The stable boundaries of that paradigm have differentiated its scope from, say, that of sociology, or psychology, or political science, and the Classical/Neo-classical from that of the Keynesian or the Marxist brand.

The Mainstream Paradigm

The core outlook of establishment economics, Alfred Marshall called it the 'organon', can be simply stated. It posits as an image of the real but also as a normative ideal, a system of rational self-seeking choice exercised by individuals interacting competitively in decentralized markets where the flow of resources is directed by free-moving price and where private ownership and control is the motivating force to efficiency. In these terms it explains production, trade and distribution in market systems.

In the two centuries since its inception, establishment economics has been greatly elaborated and refined. Numerous puzzles have been solved within its frame. It has served to explain observed phenomena, and has provided workable solutions for some problems of policy. It has never deviated in its operation from what Thomas Kuhn called 'normal science'. For two hundred years the character of the paradigm has not changed. When Samuelson wrote his *Foundations* half a century ago, he translated the propositions of the paradigm into a mathematical language so that those propositions could be challenged and possibly falsified through test of specific derivative prediction. Mathematization continued apace and mathematical virtuosity became a prerequisite to the economist's craft; but there was no challenge to and no falsification of the propositions of the paradigm through the test of specific derivative prediction.

There is this paradoxical contrast of economics and physics. The nature of the physical world has not changed in all the time and space within the scope of human observation, but, during the past two centuries there have been numerous revolutionary transformations in physics. During the past two centuries there have been revolutionary changes in the character and organizations of society, but no transformation of the economics paradigm. In the one case the reference universe remains the same, but the word concerning it and our understanding of it through physics, has been fundamentally transformed. In the other there have been fundamental transformations of the reference universe but the word concerning it and our understanding of it through establishment economics, has, for the past two centuries, remained unchanged.

In these regards, Kuhn's paradigm is, for establishment economics, a perfect fit.

Problems, Falsifications and the Development of Economic Thought

The assumption of a critical discourse that would constantly challenge and submit the basic tenets of theory to the test of specific prediction; and of failures in that test that falsify theory, and lead to the revolutionary transformation of the paradigm, are at the heart of Popper's argument. How well does this apply to the experience of economics?

In fact falsification has been at the root of all substantive developments of economic thought. But the process has not been as Popper envisaged it. Thus:

(1) The mainstream paradigm was not changed as a consequence either of these falsifications or of the new theory generated in order to transcend them.
(2) The new theory has sometimes found a place outside of the mainstream paradigm.
(3) Challenges, failures and falsifications of theory were very rarely the consequence of any critical discourse internal to the discipline, but were forced on economics from the outside.

The peculiar durability of the core theory as well as its susceptibility to basic challenge are partially explicable by the ideological character of economics and its function as a 'policy science'. As the long-standing apologia for *laissez-faire* capitalism, any attack upon or threat to the integrity of the theory is resisted as an attack on 'free enterprise'. On the same grounds the failures of the economy are considered as falsifications of the theory and the problems of the economy are forced upon the economist by the pressure of public demand. The falsification and development of theory has been rooted in social crisis rather than in any critical discourse internal to the discipline.

This can be shown by a review of the innovative developments in economic thought.

Anomalies

The economics paradigm traces an isle of the solvable in a sea of the inexplicable. It cannot account for, explain or predict a host of economic phenomena and events. With its assumption of rational, self seeking individualized choice it leaves out of account the economic consequences of variations in attitude, value, culture and ideology, or variation in the institutional context of choice, or class struggle and collective behavior. Nor, with its assumption of property as the locus of power and of ownership as that which links power to efficiency, can it explain the public economy or the economy of corporate organizations. And so on.

In some instances theories, even whole schools of thought have developed outside the paradigm to explain the effects on economic phenomena and events of these excluded variables. Thus the Institutionalist School of John R. Commons brings into account the effects of the law as the context of transaction in the determination of economic event. Or the so-called organizational theorists like Herbert Simon who try to explain the organizational choice in modern corporate enterprise in contrast to the individualized entrepreneurial choice assumed in the mainstream paradigm, where choice is assumed to operate within the frame of the proprietary firm with control based on ownership.

Depression, Mass Unemployment and Keynesian Economics

In contrast to physics, economic theories, indeed all social theories reflect realities particular to their time; and since the character of the social universe changes, their reflection of reality must become more attenuated with the passage of time. Thus Classical/Neo-Classical economics took its form in the seventeenth and eighteenth centuries, and its assumptions reflect the experience of the rural, commercial, pre-industrial societies of those days. It was an era that experienced financial 'panics'. And the theory accounts for these. But modern depression with its mass unemployment did not come until the advent of large scale industry and of the massive modern corporation.

Neo-Classical theory cannot account for, cannot even admit the logical possibility of depression and the phenomenon of sustained mass unemployment. With Say's Law it predicted exactly the opposite. The severity of these periodic visitations increased through the mid-nineteenth and into the twentieth century, culminating in the Great Depression of the 1930s. That world scale catastrophe toppled Germany and Italy into Fascism and threatened the viability of capitalism throughout the world.

Sustained mass unemployment could no longer be brushed aside as a frictional, incidental, passing deviation from the norm, but had to be recognized as a massive falsification of the theory; or at least proof positive of Neo-Classical theory's irrelevance to the great problem of the twentieth century. With the credibility of mainstream economics gone, governments turned from its guidance. Their policies broke free in *ad hoc* efforts to stave off further disaster. For them it was sink or swim. It was sink or swim too for mainstream economics. But note, this surfacing of failure and the falsification of establishment theory was not provoked by the challenges of a critical discourse. No economist selected the problem of mass unemployment as a means of disproving Neo Classical theory. The problem, and the open failure and clear falsification of the Neo Classical paradigm, was forced upon economics by public pressure.

Under this pressure and the inescapable failure of establishment economics to comprehend or to provide any rational antidote to a deadly malaise, Keynesian macroeconomics emerged. What then? Did the new theory displace and replace the old? It did not. It succeeded precisely because it did not threaten or disturb or change by an iota the Neo-Classical paradigm, but seemingly enabled mainstream economists to comprehend and grapple with the problem of mass unemployment without surrendering their commitment to that paradigm.

Ostensibly Keynesian theory was compatible with the mainstream paradigm. In truth it was not. They coexisted but as different and distant species. The two are based on fundamentally opposed premises. Keynesian theory absolutely requires price fixity, while neo-classical theory turns on the assumption of free moving price. They coexisted nevertheless until the failure of Keynesian theory to explain (and predict) stagflation, i.e., the simultaneous rise of prices and of unemployment experienced in the 1970s. Since then Keynesian theory has drifted into a sort of limbo leaving the Neo Classical paradigm without a rival.

Certainly the so-called 'Keynesian Revolution' was an innovative development in economics, the most important in a century, permanently opening new perspectives on the world. It arose out of a failure and falsification of mainstream economics, but it in no way transformed the mainstream paradigm.

Monopolistic Competition

During the same era, with Neo-Classical defences battered by its failure to account for mass unemployment, its assumptions assailed, its orthodoxy weakened, its young turks impertinent, surveys were conducted that questioned business executives concerning their accustomed practices. It was found that business practice, quite unequivocally according to the businessmen's responses to these surveys, in no way approximated what mainstream theory predicted, e.g., businesses did not price their goods and services by reference to marginal costs. Defenders of the paradigm drove these surveys from the scene on the grounds that surveys are *ipso facto* invalid as a test of behaviour. 'Watch what business does', they said, 'not what businessmen say they do'.

And what did those who watched what business did, discover?

They became aware of the painful reality of excess capacity as virtually a universal business condition during those years; wherein the capacity existed to increase production and thereby to increase profits with sales at ongoing prices. Two new and closely related theories, of 'monopolistic competition'[5] and 'imperfect competition'[6] emerged to account for this excess capacity, a phenomenon that falsified mainstream theory.

The theories of monopolistic competition and imperfect competition, claiming to describe a widespread condition in the modern economy, were developed within and were consistent with the analytic framework of Neo-Classical economics.

Thus in monopolistic competition, choice and control are exercised by rational, self-seeking, profit-maximizing individuals. Private ownership is the power source, and self-interested profit maximization is the motivating force. There are no obstructions to the entry of new firms to compete with the old. Competition is intense. Profits approximate the competitive norm. What distinguishes the firm in monopolistic competition is that it operates in a somewhat segmented market as do the builders in a particular town or as does the gas station on a particular street corner, and/or that its product or service is in some way differentiated from that of others, as are brands of toothpaste or cereals or automobiles.

The hitch was this. Under conditions of monopolistic competition where the firm possesses a real though unstable power over price, equilibrium price and output are indeterminant. Therefore to admit that such firms constitute a substantial part of the economy would rule out the possibility of a theory of general equilibrium. In the words of Sir John R. Hicks:

Yet it has to be recognized that a general abandonment of the assumption of perfect competition, a universal assumption of [monopolistic competition] must have very destructive consequences for economic theory. Under [monopolistic competition] the stability conditions become indeterminant: and the basis on which economic laws can be constructed is therefore shorn away. . . . It is, I believe, only possible to save anything from this wreck — and it must be remembered that the threatened wreckage is that of the greater part of general equilibrium theory — if we can assume that the markets confronting most firms with which we will be dealing do not differ greatly from perfectly competitive firms. . . . At least this getaway seems well worth trying. We must be aware however that we are taking dangerous steps, and probably limiting to a serious extent the problems with which our subsequent analysis will be fitted to deal.
      Value and Capital (Oxford, Clarendon Press, 1945).

The theory of monopolistic competition if accepted not only eliminates the possibility of a relevant theory of general equilibrium, it also refutes the ideologically important claim of Neo-Classical economics that under conditions of open competition, the free market system 'tends' to a condition of optimal resource allocation, with price equal to average costs at the highest possible level of organizational and operating efficiency. For these reasons the theory of monopolistic competition was not compatible with the 'received view' of establishment economics.

In the section quoted above, Sir John speaks with rare candor and prescience. He proposes that the theory of monopolistic competition be assumed away; not because it is untrue or insignificant but because otherwise it will upset his theoretical apple cart. This is precisely what happened. And Part 3 of this chapter provides a living illustration of how it happened.

The observed existence of excess capacity falsified Neo-Classical theory. In response a modification is developed to explain excess capacity and to predict its consequences, with the effect of even more completely falsifying the Neo-Classical paradigm. The theories of monopolistic/imperfect competition were never refuted; their scope and significance was never tested; they were never even strongly opposed. Their implications were simply ignored, indeed never recognized by the mass of technicians and yeoman,workers who man the ramparts of the discipline. Pigeon-holed, they never entered into the mainstream of thought, nor did they become the nucleus of another discourse.

Technology, Productivity and Development

The dynamics of Neo-Classical economics like that of Newtonian cosmology is the dynamic of the pendulum, of movements towards or away from equilibrium, of swings about a norm. It cannot account for or predict the process of development. Beyond Adam Smith's promise of a one time leap to a higher level of productivity via increased trade enabling the advantages of specialization, there was no place for economic progress in the Classical economics. The Classical economics of Ricardo and Malthus, on the contrary, predicted continuous and inevitable economic decline to the edge of universal starvation.

That prediction was radically falsified by subsequent events in the nineteenth century, when, out of a chaos of dislocation and misery, rose the colossus of industrialization with its unparalleled outpouring of wealth. And a new episteme reflected this experience of competitive struggle and evolutionary emergence, expressed in the biology of Darwin and the economics of Karl Marx. The economics of Thorstein Veblin posited the struggle between the attitudes and outlook of the engineer and the financier, of the builder versus the manipulator as the key to our economic future.

The economics of Joseph Schumpeter focused on the process of technological innovation and its consequences for the capitalist market economy. All that was outside of and excluded from the mainstream paradigm whose essential form remained as it had been.

Yet the experience of industrialization and the attacks of the Marxists not only on the truth of the theory but also on the economic system that it described and defended, could not but have some effect on the mainstream paradigm. Thus while the Malthusian and Ricardian logic and its implicit predictions remained, its conclusion was suppressed or ignored. And as an explanation of the undeniable rise of productivity and, at the same time as a defence of the system of capitalist income distribution, the supplementary theory of Bohm-Bawerk was incorporated into the Neo-Classical paradigm. This held that the rise of productivity was brought about through more 'round about or indirect' systems of production; that greater roundaboutness was the consequence of capital accumulation; that capital accumulation required saving; that saving requires capitalists who abstain from consumption; and that the profits accruing to the capitalist is a reward for his abstinence. The critical prediction then was that higher productivity was a function of capital accumulation.

Neo-Classical economic theory explains variation in real output per capita simply as a function of changing factor ratios. Reduce the ratio of capital and land per unit of labour, and output per man hour must diminish (which is Malthusian theory in a nutshell). Increase the ratio of capital and/or land per unit of labour, then output per man hour must rise. Since the quantity of land is given, the only feasible way of increasing productivity according to this theory is through the accumulation of capital. Hence the productivity of labour (as rationalized by Bohm-Bawerk) is determined by the level of capital accumulation.

A precautionary note. Capital, in Classical\Neo-Classical theory, is understood and is measured in lieu of the actual resources embodied in it, as the depreciated value of the existing stock of producer durables, e.g., factory buildings, industrial and agricultural machines and equipment. An increase in capital is not to be confused with an increase in business-oriented investment. An investment expenditure, for example, to replace one piece of equipment for another that embodied an equal amount of labour and natural resources would increase investment but not the level of accumulated capital.

Therefore the theory predicted that the enormous increase in real output per capita experienced in the United States over the span of its industrialization must have been the consequence of a corresponding increase in the quantity of real capital, i.e., in the value of durable goods per capita. In order to measure how great this causal accumulation of capital had been, Professor Moses Abramovitz organized a massive study sponsored by the National Bureau of Economic Research to correlate observed increases in output per capita and observed increases in accumulated capital per worker in the United States since 1870. The results of the Abramovitz study were published in 1956.[7]

The purpose of the study had been to measure the significance of capital accumulation. It turned out that capital accumulation was of no significance.[8] Even including as capital (*sic*) the capitalized value of land and other rents, a mere 14.5 per cent increase in output per capita could be explained by a correlated increase in capital per capita, with a 250 per cent increase in output per capita unaccounted for. When Luigi Passinetti of Cambridge University took into account the effect of rising productivity on the value of accumulated capital, he found there to have been an absolute decrease in capital per capita during this whole period of industrialization.[9]

It was an undeniable failure of prediction, a startling falsification that sent shock waves through the discipline. With what result? A refutation and transformation of the paradigm? Not at all. In response, my namesake Robert W.

Solow statistically segregated out that small part of the increase in productivity that could conceivably be accounted for as a function of capital accumulation, setting it apart from the rest.[10] The unaccounted for residual was sometimes labelled 'technology.' The dour Roy Harrod sternly relegated the consideration of anything but capital accumulation into a limbo beyond the pale of economic theory.[11] Solow's paper calmed the agitated profession by imputing some small significance to the accumulation of capital so that economists, ignoring the unexplained residual, could feel safe within the shrunken boundary of their paradigm and go about their business as before. Later, Theodore Schultz in an effort to save the threatened paradigm proposed the very equivocal notion of 'human capital', wherein expenditures on education, training, nutrition or whatever might serve to raise the work potential, should also be counted as capital accumulation.[12] Both Solow and Schultz were to receive Nobel Prizes for their contribution in preserving the status of establishment theory unruffled.

Neo-Classical theory survived unscathed. This is not to say that this decisive falsification was without practical effect. It certainly reduced the credibility of capital theory. It stimulated an interest in, and a new readiness to publish *ad hoc* studies in technology and education. And in Cambridge University a new school of thought took tentative form, in the effort to create a general theory free of the notion of capital accumulation.

What may we conclude as to the relevance of Kuhn's paradigm and Popper's canon? Perhaps, so far as economics is concerned, that both are right and both are wrong. The paradigm is real. It is indeed an association of puzzle-solvers operating within the framework of an accepted analytic apparatus, whose research offers no challenge to the paradigm. And the heroes of the profession are not those who dispose of the fallacious and open new horizons of understanding, but those who preserve establishment theory against any such threat.

On the other hand falsification counts. While a specific failure of derivative prediction is of no significance, the massive failure of the paradigm to deliver on its promises is at the source of all the significant substantive developments of economic thought. The effect has been to spawn new schools, cults, heresies, special or supplementary theories outside the paradigm and enclaves of anomaly hidden within it.

Accumulating falsifications presumably undermine the theory and the universe it pretends to encompass. That sense of widening irrelevance accounts perhaps for the burgeoning realm of the model builders. These, the purest of the puzzle-solvers with no commitment to understand experienced realities, are no part of the world of Adam Smith, David Ricardo, Karl Marx or Alfred Marshall. Their models are about nothing in particular and nothing in general, 'composed of nothing but mental constructs',[13] tautologies pure and simple.

2.   RHETORIC

McClosky's Critique of Economics and the Canon

We will examine Donald McClosky's critique of the canon in relation to economics. He identifies as the dominant methodology, dogma, outlook in economics, what he calls 'modernism'.[14]

The mark of modernism is plain in Anglo-American economics since the 1930s. Not withstanding its gleam of steely brilliance, it has produced by now many crippled economists. Many are bored by history, disdainful of other social sciences, ignorant of their civilization, thoughtless in ethics, and unreflective in method. Even the wise and good among the congregation, who are numerous, find it hard to reconcile their faith with the ceremonies required of them on Sunday.

Only religion can be like this, at once both noble and corrupting. The Ten Commandments and Golden Rule of Modernism in economics and other sciences are

1. Prediction and control is the point of science.

2. Only the observable implications (or predictions) of a theory matter to its truth.

3. Observability entails objective, reproducible experiments; mere questionnaires interrogating human subjects are useless because humans might lie.

4. If and only if an experimental implication of a theory proves false is the theory proved false.

5. Objectivity is to be treasured; subjective 'observations' (introspection) is not scientific knowledge, because the objective and the subjective cannot be linked.

6. Kelvin's Dictum: 'When you cannot express it in numbers your knowledge is of a meager and unsatisfactory kind.' And the Golden Rule (Hume's Fork): 'When we run over the libraries persuaded of these principles, what havoc must we make? If we take in hand any volume, of divinity or school metaphysics for instance, let us ask. *Does it contain any abstract reasoning concerning quantity or number?* No. *Does it contain any experimental matter concerning matter of fact and existence?* No. Commit it then to the flames: for it can contain nothing but sophistry and illusion.

Donald McClosky, *The Rhetoric of Economics* (Madison, Wisconsin, The University of Wisconsin Press, 1985) pp. 7–8.

McClosky undertakes to debunk these alleged commandments of modernism with arguments heralded by these bold black headings.

MODERNISM IS A POOR METHOD

IT IS OBSOLETE AS PHILOSOPHY

FALSIFICATION IS NOT COGENT

PREDICTION IS NOT POSSIBLE IN ECONOMICS

MODERNISM ITSELF IS NOT POSSIBLE AND IS NOT ADHERED TO

These assertions are supported, alas, by no more than a quip and a quote. Only two transcend the statement of an opinion: namely that prediction is not possible in economics and that falsification is not cogent (cogent = 'having no power to control or constrain, not appealing forcibly to the mind or reason, not valid'.) These are the two sides of a single coin for if prediction is not possible, then falsification through prediction cannot be cogent. If both or either assertion were true, that would be fatal to the positivist canon and Popper's rule. Both assertions, as stated, are false.

Every statement that the economist or economics makes about something that exists is a predictive conjecture. Because it is about something that exists, it can conceivably be checked against the facts. Statements made that are not in accord with observation count as a failed prediction; and when prediction fails then, following Popper, the statement is falsified. If economics or the economist says that population will increase so long as wages are above the level of subsistence, that prediction can be checked against the record. If economics or the economists should say that with drought and a cut in the supply of corn, its price will rise, that prediction can be checked against the record. If economics or the economist should say that to raise the tariff on a major agricultural import will raise the rent of agricultural land, that prediction can be checked against the record. If economics or the economist should say that the rate at which consumption increases lags behind the rate at which income increases, that prediction can be checked against the record. If economics or the economist should say that the firm will produce to the point where marginal costs are equal to marginal revenue, that prediction can be checked against the record. Whenever the statement is not in accord with the observable facts, then prediction fails and the statement, in Popper's terms, is falsified.

Economics and the economist have made innumerable statements about that which exists in the world. And there have been innumerable failures of prediction, innumerable falsifications. It is quite true that economists ignore such failures of prediction and that discipline resists the assault of falsification.

On the other hand, as we have seen, all of the important mutations in the corpus of economic thought (whether in producing something new or defensively finding the means of shoring up an established structure of thought whose foundations have been shaken), have been brought about by the shock of massive falsifications, and would not have occurred without such failures of prediction.

PREDICTION IS POSSIBLE

FALSIFICATION IS COGENT

And if McClosky would eliminate modernism, with what would he replace it? Not with another set of rules. For him 'any rule-bound methodology is objectionable'. Instead he offers RHETORIC. Forget the notions of truth and falsehood; such ideas are archaic and metaphysical. What matters, and all that matters, is that a statement be accepted. For that, one must persuade, and hence must master rhetoric, which is the art of persuasion.

Whatever other objections we might have to McClosky's arguments, we can agree, regarding science as a system of discourse, that 'good science is good conversation'. It is not at all clear however that McClosky's purpose is to improve and raise that level of conversation. Like the dedicated adman or the super used car salesman, he cares only for persuasiveness. If, as he demonstrates in his chapter 'The

Rhetoric of Scientism: How John Muth Persuades', scholarly dullness, heavy jargon and obscurantist ritual are persuasive, then scholarly dullness, heavy jargon and obscurantist ritual is the way to go.

McClosky proposes no substantive reform in economics. He accepts all the modelling and mathematizing. He does obeisance to its idols and leaves tribute at their shrines. Save for the elimination of the formal constraints of modernism which, in any case, are honoured only in the breach, he envisages things going on just as before. We're OK Jack, just need to shake off some excess baggage.

3. COMMITMENT TO AND EVASION OF THE CANON

A Demonstration

We hope that the discussion that follows will demonstrate the actual operation of the paradigm in the rejection or suppression of falsifications that threaten it; and the gap between pretension in the nominal commitment to the methodological rule and the rationalization of a practice in contradiction to the rule.

In 1953 Milton Friedman published his 'famous' paper on 'The Methodology of Positive Economics' as lead essay in his book *Essays in Positive Economics* (Chicago, University of Chicago Press). This sparked what became certainly one of the most intense and enduring methodological controversies in post Second World War economics.[15] In the public mind, Paul Samuelson became the other protagonist in a battle of the giants; though in fact Samuelson confined himself to short replies and comments, and Friedman never responded to his critics or further elaborated upon his short essay.

Friedman's 1953 essay divides itself, following his own dictum, into two parts. The first part is a normative statement of what ought to be the methodology of economics, with kow-tows to the philosophy of science and the requisite testing and falsification of hypothesis through prediction. Thus we read:

> Viewed as a body of substantive hypothesis, theory is to be judged for its predictive power for a class of phenomena which it is intended to 'explain.' Only factual evidence can show whether it is 'right' or 'wrong' or, better, tentatively 'accepted' as valid or 'rejected.' . . . the only relevant test of the *validity of a hypothesis is comparison of its predictions with experience.* (pp.8-9).

Elsewhere Friedman specifically aligns himself with the philosophy and the rules laid down by Karl Popper.[16]

The second, the *positive* part of Friedman's essay demonstrates his methodology in practice; for it is his purpose to attack and on methodological grounds to dispose of the new and then popular theories of monopolistic and imperfect competition, and of ongoing efforts to survey business practices.

The Defence of the Paradigm

The theories of monopolistic and imperfect competition and the efforts to study business practice directly were challenges, Friedman held, based on a denial of the 'realism' of the assumptions of Neo-Classical theory. But this, he asserts, is untenable. Theory cannot be challenged on the grounds that its assumptions are unrealistic: the only allowable test is as to whether the theory 'works' with respect to 'the class of phenomena the theory is designed to explain'. *Ergo* the theories of monopolistic and imperfect competition and the direct test of business activity and motivation are illegitimate and must be ruled out of consideration. It is thus the crux of his argument that there can be no legitimate attack on Neo-Classical (or any) theory on the grounds that its assumptions are unrealistic.

Misunderstanding about this apparently straightforward process centers on the phrase 'The class of phenomena the hypothesis is intended to explain.' The difficulty in social sciences of getting new evidence for this class of phenomena and of judging its conformity with the implications of hypothesis makes it tempting to suppose that other more readily available evidence is equally relevant to the validity of the hypothesis — to suppose that hypotheses have not only 'implications' but also 'assumptions' and the conformity of these 'assumptions' to 'reality' is a test of the validity of the hypothesis *different from* or *additional* to the test by implications. This widely held view is fundamentally wrong . . .

In so far as a theory can be said to have 'assumptions' at all, and in so far as their 'realism' can be judged independently of the validity of the predictions, the relation between the significance of a theory and the 'realism' of its 'assumptions' is almost the opposite of that suggested by the view under criticism. Truly important and significant hypotheses will be found to have 'assumptions' that are wildly inaccurate descriptive representations of reality, and, in general, the more significant the theory, the more unrealistic the assumptions (in this sense). [p. 14]

In order to demonstrate that in the natural as well as in the social sciences assumptions are unrealistic, and that this lack of realism in the assumptions of theory is irrelevant for prediction-falsification, Friedman offers two examples from the natural sciences.

He proposes the following as an example allegedly analogous 'to many hypotheses in the social sciences.'

Consider the density of leaves around a tree. I suggest the hypothesis that the leaves are positioned as if each leaf deliberately sought to maximize the amount of sunlight it receives, given the position of its neighbors, as if it knew the physical laws determining the amount of sunlight that would be received in various positions and could move rapidly or instantaneously from any one position to any other desired and unoccupied position. [p. 19]

We note that the hypothesis proposed by Friedman consists of two distinct statements:

(1) that leaves are positioned so as to maximize the sunlight each leaf receives, given the position of its neighbours,
(2) that this positioning is as if each leaf deliberately seeks to maximize the amount of sunlight it receives given the position of its neighbours, and as if it knew the physical laws determining the amount of sunlight that would be received in various positions and could move rapidly or instantaneously from any one position to any other desired and unoccupied position.

Friedman takes the second statement as the 'assumption'. He derides that assumption as unrealistic ('so far as we know, leaves do not "deliberate" or consciously "seek", have not been to school or learned the relevant laws of science or the mathematics required to calculate the "optimum" position, and cannot move from position to position', p. 20). Allegedly the hypothesis is not rendered invalid because of that unrealistic assumption. Therefore, he concludes, the assumptions of physical science are unrealistic but that lack of realism does not affect the validity of theory.

He proposes, as another example, 'the law of falling bodies. It is an accepted hypothesis that the acceleration of a body dropped in a vacuum is a constant'. He proceeds to spell out the formula. Again the statement breaks down into two parts: (1) if bodies fall in a vacuum, i.e., if they fall in the absence of intervening variables (2) they will fall at a constant, predetermined rate of acceleration. He then notes that a feather dropped on a windy day will not fall at that stipulated rate of acceleration. From this he deduces (1) that the assumption (or the whole hypothesis?) is unrealistic, and (2) that it is impossible to deny the viability of a theory by reference to its unrealistic assumptions.

What are 'Assumptions?'

While offering no specific definition of 'assumptions', Friedman speaks of 'crucial assumptions' as 'key elements of the abstract model'. He associates assumptions with postulates (p.26), and sees the assumptions as interchangeable with the implications of theory (p. 27). For a theory of oligopolistic behaviour he gives as an example of 'assumptions', 'that entrepreneurs seek to maximize their returns by any means including acquiring or extending monopoly power'. Accepting this, we can infer at least that the assumptions of a theory, like that concerning the motivation of entrepreneurs, are generalizations about some sphere of observable realities. If assumptions are so understood, then Friedman's examples from natural science not only do not support his argument, they suggest the very opposite; that the assumptions integral to a valid theory in the physical science must be realistic.

He takes as a proof that unrealistic assumptions do not invalidate hypothesis in the physical sciences, the fact that we do not dismiss the hypothesis concerning positioning of leaves because the phrase *'as if* each leaf deliberately sought . . . *as if* it knew the physical laws determining . . .' is not a realistic statement. Except that the 'as if' phrase is not an empirical statement about what occurs or exists. It is a metaphor. Because it is not an empirical statement about reality it cannot predict concerning reality, hence it cannot be refuted by any test of such prediction. If, however, the 'as if' phrase was worded as an empirical statement about that which exists, and as an assumption integral to an hypothesis about that which exists; if for example the hypothesis was given as:

> Consider the density of leaves around a tree. I suggest the hypothesis that the leaves are positioned as they are because each leaf deliberately seeks to maximize the amount of sunlight it receives, given the position of its neighbors, because it knows the physical laws determining the amount of sunlight that would be received in various positions and can move rapidly or instantaneously from any one position to any other desired and unoccupied position.

Then, any scientist worth his salt would immediately invalidate the hypothesis and its assumptions, precisely because they are unrealistic.

Concerning the law of falling bodies, 'It is an accepted hypothesis that the acceleration of a body dropped in a vacuum is a constant'. Since a feather on a windy day will not drop at the postulated rate of acceleration, Friedman calls the assumption ('in a vacuum') unrealistic. This is taken as proof that it is impossible to test a theory by reference to its (inherently unrealistic) assumptions. Except that 'in a vacuum' is not assumption about the world. It does not state that which exists or occurs. It is simply a standard for measurement. If, however, 'in a vacuum' was reformulated as a statement about that which exists and made into an assumption integral to the law of falling bodies: if, for example, it was stated that bodies everywhere fall at the same constant rate of acceleration because the world is a vacuum, then any scientist worth his salt would invalidate the hypothesis in an instant precisely because the assumption of a universal vacuum was unrealistic.

Gravitational force is assumed in the theory of planetary motion. Following Friedman, as an assumption it is immune from the test of prediction. And no legitimate prediction independently inferred from, and testing the validity of statements concerning the force of gravitation is allowable. The only prediction allowable for gravitation and other elements of Newtonian theory, would be in relation to planetary motion. In fact, gravity and other elements in the Newtonian system, are boundlessly and independently tested through inferential prediction. Should they fail to meet the test and hence be shown unrealistic, that would falsify the 'assumption' as well as the larger theory.

If one understands assumptions as empirical statements about observable reality, holding with Samuelson (1963) that a theory is 'a set of axioms, postulates, or hypotheses that stipulate something about observable reality [otherwise it is] not economics . . . or anything that can properly be called science',[17] then Friedman's argument is absurd. What is interesting is the mode in which the consequence of a prediction and falsification of the theory is evaded, not as a denial but in the name of commitment to the methodology of prediction and falsification.

What means 'Realistic?'

What is or is not realistic?

I understand realistic to mean congruent with reality, consistent with that universe of experienced reality to which the statement refers, with prediction serving as a test of that congruence. To say therefore that a statement is unrealistic is simply a shorthand way of saying that statement obviously, self-evidently cannot meet the test of prediction.

But consider Friedman's words in the text of the chapter, where he attempts to establish that the assumptions of theory must, *ipso facto*, be unrealistic, and the more wildly inaccurate the assumptions, the more significant the theory. The reason for this, we are told, 'is simple'.

A hypothesis is important if it 'explains' much by little, that is, if it abstracts the common and crucial elements from the mass of complex and detailed circumstances surrounding the phenomena to be explained and permits valid predictions on the basis of them alone. To be important, therefore, a hypothesis must be descriptively false in its assumptions; it takes account of, and accounts for, none of the many other attendant circumstances, since its very success shows them to be irrelevant for the phenomena to be explained. [pp. 14–15]

He appears here to give the term realistic a quite different meaning than we have attributed to it; the realistic seems to have been equated to the totally descriptive. Ernest Nagel commented on this notion that:

A statement can be said to be 'unrealistic' because it does not give an 'exhaustive' description of some object, so that it mentions only some traits actually characterizing the object but ignores an endless number of other traits also present. However no finitely long statement can possibly formulate the totality of traits embodied in any concretely existing thing . . . . it is with this rather trivial sense of the word in mind that Friedman seems frequently to defend the legitimacy of unrealistic assumptions in economic theory;

E. Nagel, 'Assumptions on Economic Theory', p. 214.

Hence the argument.

Realistic = Totally Descriptive.
The abstract is the converse of the descriptive.
The more abstract, the less descriptive.

The more encompassing and general a statement, the more abstract it becomes.

Therefore the more general, hence the more significant a statement, the more abstract and the less descriptive it will be.

The assumptions of theory are abstract statements, hence like all abstractions, they are unrealistic.

Therefore a theory cannot be challenged on the grounds that its assumptions are unrealistic since this has nothing to do with its significance or relevance.

If one equates the realistic to the totally descriptive, there is then nothing wrong with this logic. But to take this as the meaning of the term makes Friedman's argument *vis-à-vis* assumptions and predictions, even more bizarre than before.

If this is the meaning of realistic, then why confine the argument only to the assumptions. Theory, hypothesis, being even more abstract are even less descriptive, even more unreal than their assumptions and therefore should be insulated from challenge on the same priori grounds. Indeed, no empirical statement can ever be totally descriptive. Given this notion of the realistic, we are left with empty hands. Nothing that can be said about the world, is ever realistic.

Prediction as a means of testing the relation of statement and reality, makes nonsense of the very notion of the totally descriptive. Suppose as an 'assumption' I say that the trees in Yosemite National Park are made of wood. Is that unrealistic? One can infer from the statement (hence predict) that a cross sectional slice taken from any of those trees and submitted to chemical analysis, would turn out to be of cellulose. If that is done and the material collected is indeed cellulose, then the 'prediction' has been verified and offers evidence of the correctness of the statement. If it turns out that the tested material is steel or glass, then the statement is falsified. Certainly the phrase 'are made of wood' is not totally descriptive of the trees in Yosemite. It says nothing and claims nothing concerning their shape, or their height, or their foliage, or their germination and growth etc. But unrealistic?

What Happened to Prediction?

A theory in the social or in the natural sciences is a set of empirical statements, integrated as a system or model, about experienced reality; hence subject to the test of inferential prediction. Inferential prediction is simply a way of corroborating the statement with observable reality. The theory must stand as a whole. And also it must stand on the validity of its parts. There is no way to determine beforehand the facets of reality that will be illumined through exploratory predictions inferred from whatever aspects of the theory, nor through what facet the theory will encounter its limits and be falsified through inferential prediction.

PREDICTION is emblazoned on the masthead of Friedman's methodology, prediction as the sole criterion of verity, and as the sole instrument of falsification. But what happens to prediction in his practice?

Neither the theories of monopolistic nor of imperfect competition, as Friedman's substantive targets, were attacks on Neo-Classical theory or on its 'assumptions' as insufficiently descriptive, hence as unrealistic. They responded to a sense that the theory was wrong and, based on the observation of 'excess capacity', that it failed the test of inferential prediction.

Neo-Classical theory postulates an economy controlled through the choices of rational, quasi-omniscient entrepreneurs who in every case and for every facet of business choice, follow the marginal calculus. As a test of this statement it could reasonably be inferred, hence predicted that these rational and quasi-omniscient entrepreneurs would know what they were doing, would be conscious of the character of their choices, and would so organize their accounting and research procedures as to provide the information needed in order to know the marginal costs or benefits attributable to particular decisions. A series of studies based on the reports of these decision-makers found that they did not knowingly conduct their businesses on marginalist principles, and that their accounting and research procedures were not designed to supply them with the information required for the rational practice of marginalism.[18] Again a failure of prediction and a falsification of the theory.

But Friedman does not respond to these challenges of predictive failure. He makes no attempts to test and falsify their claims. He simply refuses to recognize failed prediction or even the possibility of failed prediction. All that can be properly questioned is 'whether the hypothesis works for the phenomena it purports to explain'. (p. 30) This phrase is crucial. It means that a theory should be asked only the questions it is 'designed' to answer, that its predictions should be confined to inferences it is designed accurately to predict. If prediction does not 'work', then, priori, the prediction must relate to phenomena the theory is not 'designed to explain'. It becomes, therefore, logically impossible ever to falsify and dislodge an established theory through inferential prediction.

And what is Neo-Classical economics 'designed to explain'? It is designed to explain hence, following Friedman, the optimizing, profit-maximizing behavior of the firm. But this, as Herbert Simon states, is precisely what cannot be falsified through the test of prediction:

X — businessmen desire to maximize profits; Y — businessmen can and do make the calculations that identify the profit-maximizing course of action. The theory at the market level may be summed up as: Z — prices and quantities are observed at those levels which maximize the profits of the firms in the market . . . Friedman asserts that it doesn't matter if X and Y are false, provided Z is true. . . . Most critics have accepted Friedman's assumption that proposition Z is the empirically tested one, while X and Y are not directly observable. This, of course, is nonsense. No one has, in fact, observed whether the actual positions of business firms are the profit-maximizing ones; nor has anyone proposed a method of testing this proposition by direct observation.[19]

'Problems of Methodology', *American Economic Review*,
May 1963, pp. 229–30.

The Last Word

The criticisms made of Friedman's essay, in my opinion, destroyed the entire edifice of Friedman's argument. Indeed after the first round Friedman's defenders had ceased to defend Friedman's statements, and instead levelled their attack against Samuelson's *ad hoc* critique. But even though Friedman's essay was left in shambles, it appears that the profession favoured his position over that of his critics, for he said what his auditors wanted to hear.

Thus in his 1965 comment, Samuelson notes that the communications published in the *American Economic Review* as part of the controversy, were only the tip of the iceberg of the communications received, and that:

A Gallup poll count of the mail would seem to show that there is a widespread will to disbelieve my rather hard-boiled insistence upon 'theory' as (strategically simplified) descriptions of observable and refutable empirical regularities.

The foot soldiers of every profession prefer comfort to truth; and Friedman was offering them a very comforting package. Under the cover of scientific respectability they could dismiss and ignore all threats to the established paradigm and to their habitual modes of thought.

In another respect Friedman and his cohort won the debate hands down. If never disproved or discredited, the theories of imperfect and monopolistic competition were pushed to the periphery of the discourse and beyond, and were buried there. By some unspoken consensus, the use of questionnaires to test the claims of Neo-Classical theory was tabooed in economics; though it remained operative in the separate enclave of 'organizational theory.'

What has been Demonstrated?

1.   Our review of the 'assumptions controversy' demonstrates the force of Thomas Kuhn's insistence on the inertial force of the paradigm and its resistance to contradiction and refutation. We observe the cunning of that resistance and its ability to rationalize any contradiction.

2.   While the protagonists initially and on the surface acknowledge the logic and authority of the canon; none in practice, neither Friedman nor his critics, employing different rationales and stratagems, will follow Popper's rule.

Without the rule, what then?

There is the crux of our problem. For there now exists no reasoned expectations and no accepted and practised criterion for the acceptance or rejection, the verification and falsification of statement and for the evaluation of alternative theory in the social sciences.

The failure to follow Popper's rule in spite of a nearly universal commitment to do so, is not due to the perversity of economists. It is because, for social science, the rule is inherently unworkable. We are not physics. We cannot be like physics. In fact these days it is difficult to say what physics is like. We need rules nevertheless, for a disciplined discourse, for the acceptance or rejection of statement, for a reasoned debate; but based upon what economics is and what it requires in its particular pursuit of truth. In Chapter 4 we will explain why Popper's rule is inherently unworkable in the social sciences, and we shall begin to formulate an alternative.

4

Social Science, Policy Science

This chapter will emphasize, as characteristics that determine the character of, and the rules appropriate for the discourse of economics, its reference universe as a social science, and its role as a critical component of the political system as a policy science.

PARTICULARITIES

Those decades ago at the London School of Economics I was convinced that Popper's vision of things truly portrayed practice in the physical sciences. I believed that's the way it was in physics and that physics was the model of what all the sciences should be. It was my great discovery, I thought, that economics, and, for the same reasons, the other social sciences had never and never could operate that way. Physics was at one pole and economics at the other, with no possibility of overlap. We were not like physics; could never be like physics; and, without reference to physics, we must find a way that was right for ourselves.

I now see things differently; not because I have come to think that economics is really like physics, but rather that physics, far from the canon, is not unlike the indeterminant and purpose-oriented economics I have known. There are, nevertheless, important differences between the sciences and also differences between the facets of a particular science, warranting the particularization of methodology and its rules. Each of the disciplines has the epistemological task of tailoring for itself a methodology that takes account of the character of the universe to which its categories of statement refers. In physics, for example, there are differences between the criteria of credibility and the methodology appropriate for quantum mechanics, classical mechanics, thermodynamics and cosmology. And also that takes into account its organizational character and 'purpose'. It matters for an appropriate methodology whether physics operates as a 'pure science' in academia, or as R&D in corporate and governmental laboratories.

'STUFF' OF THE REFERENCE UNIVERSE

One purpose of every science is to generalize concerning its reference universe. It could hardly be a science unless there were regularities sufficient to enable significant generalization. A first question then. Are such generalizing statements true or false? acceptable or unacceptable? Are they *credible* or not?

The philosophy of science has been primarily concerned with the rule for establishing the credibility of statement. And, as we have seen, while Popper's criterion of falsification may work well enough in the world of classical mechanics, it does not suit the micro universe of quantum mechanics where another criterion of credibility has come to prevail. The rules are different because the 'stuff' to which they refer is different.

What is the nature of the 'stuff' to which the statements of economics refer? It is a reference universe that contains and combines the constituents of each of Karl Popper's three worlds. Statements generalizing, say, about resource depletion, or about diminishing marginal return and the rent of land, fall into the physical domain of World One. Statements about alternative market structures, or the operation of a central bank, or tariffs and trade quotas or taxation and income distribution refer to the institutional constituents of the Third World.

But it is the Second World of the psyche that is the creative root of all institutional formations, of all choice and behaviour by individuals and groups. The image, the idea, the memory, the value, the belief, the conceptualization, the commitment, the ambition, the aspiration, the expectation, the need, that belong in the mind's domain is the ultimate 'stuff' of the social universe. It is a stuff without weight, quantity or measure, absolutely different from physical matter. It comes out of nowhere and vanishes without residual. And yet as we witness in the instance of *perestroika* and *glasnost* in the Soviet Union, a shift and change in that invisible stuff can, seemingly in an instant, collapse and transform a whole vast structure of social institutions and organization.

The significant regularities of the social universe, on which generalization and prediction depend, are not, as in physics, functions of determined or of random relationships. They are functions of the very opposite; of human freedom expressed in reason and in purpose.

It is essential to consider and grasp the character of this stuff in contrast to that of the physical universe, in order to fashion a methodology appropriate for the social sciences.

Besides the character of the reference universe, an appropriate methodology for the social sciences will depend on the function or functions of the science *qua* system.

POLITICAL ECONOMY AS A SYSTEM

Consider, for instance, microbiology. As a 'pure science,' it is organized to comprehend, to provide information concerning, to generalize in relation to its particular reference universe. But microbiology is also a component of the more encompassing system of 'medical research', which operates to comprehend, to generalize, to provide information relevant to the physical ailments of man, the cure, control and prevention of disease and the preservation of health. And medical research, in turn, is an element in the larger system of medicine, operating for the purpose of comprehending, controlling, preventing, curing disease and preserving human health.

The practising physician, the clinician, the pharmacist, those engaged in pharmaceutical research and those engaged in the production and promotion and sale of drugs and those engaged in their testing and control, and those engaged in the development and sale of diagnostic hardware, and those engaged in the administration and control of hospitals, and in the allocation of public monies in their support, and the psychologist and the psychoanalyst and the immunologist and the epidemiologist and the microbiologist on and on, have a role to play in this encompassing system of medicine. And yet for each the character of discourse and the nature of statement will not be the same. And the rules that control their statements and their practice will be different. And the effective operation of medicine as an integral system will require that there be rules, overt or covert, serving to coordinate and control its elements.

Economics has been considered and to a degree has developed as a pure science with its purpose to provide information, formulated as generalized statements, i.e., as theories and hypotheses, concerning the phenomena within the boundaries of a paradigm. The pure science of economics is a part of political economy, understood as a system geared to the formation and implementation of economic policy. Economics and political economy in turn are components of an encompassing political system for the exercise of public choice in the control over the affairs of a society.

THE ROLE OF SOCIAL SCIENCE IN A DEMOCRATIC POLITY

The role of the social sciences, more particularly of political economy, will differ depending upon the nature of the political system of which it is a part. In Western democracies one might break the political system into five parts:

(1) the electoral function, mobilized to hold an elected government responsive to the values, interests, needs of the electorate,
(2) the legislative function operating within the parameters of electoral preference and political commitment, to formulate policy and enact it into law,
(3) the implementation of policy via the judiciary and other agencies of the state,
(4) the measurement and assessment of the consequences and results of policy and its implementation,
(5) the critical and creative redesign of policies and of the instruments and techniques of implementation.

Many groups, many interests, many skills are involved in every step of the system; the voters, the lobbyists, the campaign contributors, the parties, the media, the elected and appointed officials, the judges and jurors and lawyers, the private contractors to public agencies, the public bureaucrats and professionals. Among them, the contribution of the social sciences is peculiarly important in modern democracy.

The problems confronting the modern state are complex beyond casual appraisal and the scope of practical experience. And, given the size and complexity of modern public or corporate organizations and the world context in which they operate, the uninstructed individual is unable to frame their rationale even from a working niche within their operation. What a creative response to the problem, say, of deteriorating environment, of laggard industry, of agricultural crisis, of stagflation, or crime and punishment, requires is deep and dedicated inquiry by persons educated for the task and detached from the pressures that harness public and corporate officialdom to a treadmill of decision-taking, hence with time to gather, to study and reflect upon the data of experience, to discuss and debate it and to test their theories concerning it, in order to comprehend and to deal creatively with those immensely complex economic and social problems, to evaluate objectively the performance of the system, and to critique and redesign its instruments or techniques of choice and implementation. No others in modern society than the academics of social sciences are presently equipped for that task.

That they alone have the necessary time and freedom and skills is not to suppose that they are doing what needs to be done or that anyone is. This, nevertheless, would seem the mission of the 'policy sciences'.

COMPONENTS OF POLITICAL ECONOMY[1]

That they might gear into the formation of policy, the generalizing theories of economics must be coupled with the selection of goals and priorities, and the evaluation of costs and benefits. Which belongs to a normative discourse to develop and debate over these and value-based systems of choice.

Then, in the frame of knowledge and of norm, a coherent and consistent set of policies requires that the *what is* and the *what ought to be* are wedded into yet another form of statement: ideology.

Beyond the formation of policy and the exercise of collective choice, is the need to fashion and develop technologies for the implementation of policy, for the control and evaluation of operations, and for the re-evaluation of policy and choice.

We will try to map out these areas of discourse. They overlap. Certainly they need not be set apart in the individual's thinking nor segregated by disciplinary enclaves. But for purposes of analysis, the differences are critical. We will call them (a) General Theory, (b) Normative

Theory, (c) Ideology and Strategy, (d) Technology and Tactic. Our intention is not to describe what now exists as organized activity, but what would be appropriate for the rational organization of a policy science.

GENERAL THEORY

Given the complexity of the problems at issue, in order to grasp the relevant political, behavioural, institutional, psychological and economic realities of modern society, an infinity of detail must be fitted into a conceptual framework and reduced to a set of significant regularities. There is no making sense of it otherwise. An endless and endlessly unique stream of phenomena and events must be dealt with *in general*, generalized. Only thus can there be provided an overview of this moving stream of phenomena and events as a basis for public choice. It would be the task of general theory in the social sciences (and of economics in the political economy) to provide the most inclusive overview possible of some class of social phenomena, and in so doing, *qua* policy science, to provide the informational base for an overall posture in the formation of public policy.

NORMATIVE THEORY

Information, no matter how general and accurate, will not suffice for public choice and the formation of policy. Every decision, every policy, whether private or public, must have its purpose, and a purpose is always the expression of values. While general theory might be useful in deducing the consequences of policy alternatives, it provides no basis for evaluating those alternatives. To critically examine, to evaluate, to propose, to critique, to expose, to reject the variety of purposes and goals and the values from which they presumably derive, calls for a discourse directed to the question of 'what ought to be?' What ought to be the objectives of public policy? What ought to be taken into account in its formation? By what criteria and measure to reckon the benefits and detriments of public choice? A normative discourse would explore such questions. The progressive evolution of policy depends upon a deepening both of moral sensibilities and of the information base. It would be the task of normative discourse to develop and inform a value consensus, to forge social purpose, to question and challenge social drift and social policy, and to evolve acceptable value criteria for the guidance of public choice in the formulation of priorities, in the weighing and balancing of social sacrifice and social purpose, in the determination of rights and the redress of wrongs.

The key statements of general theory are empirical, referring to ' that . . . out there', presumably subject to common observation and shared experience, that can conceivably be falsified by reference to shared experience. At the core of a normative discourse are statements of another order. They are not empirical. They cannot be falsified by experimental trial. They are expressive of what is felt within; and more, they express as an imperative an interior sense and belief in what ought to be.

IDEOLOGY AND STRATEGY

Suppose one has a reasonable comprehension of some sphere of social behaviour and event; and also a firmly established set of moral convictions and social values. That of itself does not answer the great and perennial question. 'What is to be done?' For that, values and knowledge must be coupled and moulded into an ideology, i.e., a goal, a purpose, an idea of what ought to be developed and made compatible with an understanding as to what exists as the base of action and change. The road we plan must have a place to go, a goal; but also it must be mapped by reference to what we know of the existing terrain. For the goal, normative theory is a reference base, and general theory offers a knowledge of the terrain. Ideology is the map.

A POLITICAL TECHNOLOGY

Suppose that general theory and its overview, and normative theory and its values are melded into an ideology and a strategy geared to a particular field of choice and action, and are fed into the process of public choice, so that a policy emerges. There remains the matter of implementing that policy. What then becomes at issue and a proper subject for discourse is *technique*. Policy is given. The question now is 'how to?' How to raise revenues? How to control aggregate expenditure? How to achieve racial integration? How to control immigration? How to police the airways? How to promote industrial development? How to improve the process of collective choice? How to improve the surveillance and the efficiency of public operations? How better to organize the discourse of policy science?

Though general theory, normative theory and ideology may remain as a reference base, the discourse would have shifted to the critique of an organization, of an operation, of a process, of a method. Creativity would be in devising concrete alternatives to the mode of action and organization. The focus is on the technology of public action and public choice with the social scientist playing the role of the social engineer.

In the chapter that follows these areas will be examined more closely and the rules appropriate to their discourse will be considered. But first a general rule for all the areas of discourse proper to the policy sciences.

TO JUDGE A POLICY SCIENCE.

We have sketched out the components of a discourse oriented to the formation and implementation of public policy. Is it worth the effort to propose this or any such schemata as a model for the re-evaluation and reorganization of social science? That question requires another.

Should social science be judged and evaluated by its contribution to the formation and implementation of public policy. Check your response in the appropriate space.

YES

NO

DON'T CARE

THE RULE OF SOCIAL PURPOSE

Whatever your answer, you have not and you cannot avoid making a value judgment.

Those who respond in the affirmative must conceive of political economy, with economics as one of its components, as a policy science geared into the political system, to be judged by its contribution to the formation and implementation of public policies.

Hence that the aim of political economy is to produce more beneficent solutions to the real and prevailing social problems of our societies; and that its organization and governance should be shaped to that end.

This, *the rule of social purpose* I propose as a general rule for the policy sciences, against which practice should be evaluated.

Given the rule of social purpose, consider the need for another rule: that which governs the admissibility of statement into the economics discourse.

THE ADMISSIBILITY OF STATEMENT

Every science, from physics to psychology, from genetics to cosmology, indeed any disciplined discourse understood as an ordered exchange of statements, may be open ended – but none are open sided. All are about something, but none are about anything. For each there are boundaries, and only certain statements are admitted into the discourse. By what criterion is statement admitted or excluded? How is the line drawn between 'This is' and This is not' economics or political science or psychology or sociology? What lays down the boundaries of the discourse?

ADMISSION BY RULE OF THE PARADIGM

The generally prevailing criterion that determines the admissibility of statement in economics and in other sciences could be called the rule of the paradigm. Following this rule, only statements that derive from, are commensurable with or incremental to the established assumptions, theories, models and analytic techniques that constitute the established paradigm can be admitted into the discourse. Other statements are excluded, not because they are wrong or uninteresting; not because they are irrelevant to or without significance in answering the burning questions or solving the real problems at hand; but because they are 'not economics', 'not physics', 'not psychology', 'not political science'. Interesting or not, relevant or not, there is no place for them here.

Through the application of this rule, the paradigm is preserved and perpetuated. It is a rule that obtains its inertial force from the universal attachment to habituated practice and inculcated modes of thought, and from the self-interest of practitioners in preserving a body of knowledge from which their authority derives and acquired skills that are their professional stock in trade.

The problem of the rule is that it blocks the entry of all significant novelty, excluding the possibility of scientific revolution, throwing up a barrier against any substantive transformation and development of a science from within. Given the effective application of the rule, the discipline cannot but go on being what it has been.

On the other hand it needs to be recognized that the rule has a positive value. It assures the coherence and continuity of a discourse spread out in space and time and drawing into itself participants from a variety of cultures. It fosters the transgenerational learning from a shared body of thought with a stable system of signs essential for effective communication, so that participants speak together in a common tongue and from the same reference base. Thereby it protects the integrity of the discipline and the coherence of the enterprise from the possibly shattering effect of a random introduction of novelty.

AN ALTERNATIVE TO THE RULE OF THE PARADIGM

There is no necessity attaching to the rule of the paradigm. It is the product not of an aware and rational choice but of drift. We have the right consciously to question its exclusionary role and to replace it with a preferred alternative. Can we devise a rule for the admissibility of statement, that will at once preserve a sufficient degree of continuity in the discourse and coherence in the enterprise, while yet enabling the entry into the discourse of statement from outside the boundaries of the paradigm that might contribute to the more beneficent solution of the real problems of society, conforming with the rule of social purpose.

To that end I propose the following.

Let the discipline be defined by its problems. Rather than on an established set of assumptions and theories,let it find its continuity in focusing on the same, open-ended set of problem areas, e.g., on the quest for full employment, for price stability, for higher productivity, for a rising real GNP, on the problems of trade imbalance, of resource depletion, of income distribution. Let it find its identity not in the presuppositions and analytic apparatus with which the cohort begins but in the policy problems on which they vector. And let any statement that is demonstrably relevant to the solution of those problems or to the formation of a policy geared to their solution, be admissible into the discourse.

Surely there will be radical changes in the phenomena encompassed by and in the nature of the crisis associated with any such set of open-ended problem areas, e.g., brought about through change in market operations, in demographic patterns, in industrial organizations, in managerial developments, in corporate restructuring, in political policies, in technology and its potential, in power shifts, in ideological confrontations, in cultural transformations, in international and intergroup relations, in climatic conditions, in natural catastrophes, in resource availabilities, etc., Hence the theories and the variables and the analytic techniques relevant to the formation of policies must also change; and correspondingly the substantive content and focus of the discourse. Experience suggests, however, that the substantive character of the reference universe of any of these open-ended problem areas changes with a sufficient degree of evolutionary continuity to enable an evolutionary continuity in the development of the discourse as well.

THE UNITY OF THE SCIENCES

We have tried to demonstrate the particularity of the individual sciences, to refute the notion that they can be subordinated to a universal rule, and the need to tailor epistemologies to the unique character of each. And yet we must also seek to understand the relationships of each to the others as parts of an integral whole. Popper tried to do this through his three worlds where human freedom, physical determinance and social institutions share a place as constituents of the whole.

With due respect to Popper's effort, his three worlds are a grab bag that may contain but can explain neither the relationship of the parts nor the operations of the whole. We will venture a far too abbreviated summary of an alternative approach that is more fully developed in my *Economic Organizations and Social Systems* (1969) and *The Political Authority and the Market System* (1975).

The critical contrast and linkage is between the systems of the individual psyche and those of the social organization; more specifically between the functional, cognitive and value structures of the psyche, and the parallel cognitive, cultural and functional systems of the social organization.

We conceive of society as the complex interaction of functional systems, cognitive systems, and cultural systems. Functional systems integrate the activities of different individuals into the provision of some valued good(s) or service(s), e.g., markets, governments, families, churches, corporations, armies.

Cognitive systems produce, accumulate, disseminate, inculcate information and serve in the solution and resolution of empirical problems and puzzles. They are embodied in artefact and institutions, e.g.,in electronic networks and computer software, in languages, in books and in libraries and in schools, in the media, in the calculus, in scientific theories and in the science disciplines. While they must operate through functional organizations, they infiltrate all functional systems and yet develop independently of functional activities.

Cultural systems operate as instruments of evaluation, and in the generation, inculcation, challenge, replacement and transformation of values. Like cognitive systems, cultural systems are embodied in institutions and artefacts, in bibles, codes and laws, in religions, in churches, in parliaments and in the judiciary, in literature, in museums, in street gangs. They too operate through functional organizations, e.g., in the political evaluation of and choice between policy alternatives, in the prioritization of policy objectives, in the administration of justice, in the distribution of income, in the selection of problems and areas for scientific inquiry, in the production of, challenges to, inculcation and perpetuation of a prevailing table of values. In some form or other they infiltrate all functional systems, and yet develop independently of their functional activities.

The functional, cognitive, cultural systems of society have their counterpart in the functional, cultural cognitive components of the individual psyche. To use Jean Piaget's term, cognitive systems of society have their analogue in the knowledge mastered, the information accumulated, the theories learned, the analytic skills acquired and the problem-solving capabilities of the cognitive structures of the psyche. The cultural systems of society have their counterpart in the beliefs, commitments, and capacity for evaluation of what we would call the value structures of the individual psyche.

And ideology.

Ideology, understood as a coherent set of ideas as to what is and what ought to be with respect to some area of individual or social activity and choice, is the interface between the individual and society, between the functional, cultural and cognitive complex, and the individual psyche that both acts and is acted upon by that complex. On one side, ideology is the individual's eye on his world, the nexus through which he comprehends and participates in the functional activities of society and in its process of evaluation and choice. On the other, it is the inculcation and the reshaping of ideologies that society forms, directs, controls and mobilizes the energy of the individual. And yet ideologies have their creative root in the individual psyche; and through its power to question, challenge, displace a prevailing ideology the individual can act to transform society.

In these terms one can comprehend the interaction of social systems, including the systems of science,as parts of an integral whole; and perhaps explain important phenomena as Michel Foucault explained the revolutionary transformations of science, and as I have tried to explain the industrial revolution, and the evolution of constitutional law in the United States.

5

The Character of the Discourse

EMPIRICAL STATEMENT AND GENERAL THEORY IN SOCIAL SCIENCE

We refer to statements such as these:

- Population will increase whenever wages are higher than the income needed for subsistence.
- When population increases in relation to the available land, productivity declines.
- Productivity increases through capital accumulation.
- Capital accumulation accelerates through individual saving.
- Entrepreneurs increase production until marginal costs equals marginal revenue. They invest to the point where marginal yield equals the rate of interest.
- The rise in consumption spending lags behind the rise in the level of income, and the higher the level of aggregate spending the lower the proportion of consumption expenditure.
- Class struggle is the dynamic force that accounts for all social and economic change and development.
- Power corrupts; and absolute power corrupts absolutely.

These are statements about an objective reality that is observable and observed. Hence they are empirical statements. And they are general statements, open-ended, applying to any event that conforms with their specifications or that can be deduced therefrom. Empirical and generalizing, they belong to the discourse of General Theory.

And how shall we decide whether such statements are true or false? What should be our criterion of credibility? I take it as axiomatic that their truth or falsehood should be tested against the universe of events and phenomena to which they refer. But how?

According to the canon, the failure of an event to conform in every precise detail with a specific prediction accurately deduced from a generalizing statement, falsifies that statement. Hence a statement is credible if it has been frequently and freely submitted to the test of specific prediction and has not yet been falsified. That criterion presupposes a universe of determined relationships, relationships that do not change; where what has once been properly identified, the hydrogen atom for example, retains the qualities by which it was identified; where if A co-joined with B produces C then, parameters given, A's co-joined with B's will produce C's throughout. The reference universe of classical physics meets these preconditions, and a general statement in classical physics would be falsified (though not necessarily discarded) by the failure in any detail of a prediction accurately inferred from that statement.

The reference universe of quantum mechanics does not meet these preconditions, and here the test is in the prediction of a probability. But to accept this test as a criterion of credibility requires the assumption that the distribution of event (or the table of probability) is constant, continuing, consistent.

EMPIRICAL STATEMENT IN SOCIAL SCIENCE

What of the universe of social phenomena and event to which the statements of general theory in the social sciences refer? Consider. Individual and group behaviour and all the policies and all the institutions of society have their source in and are functions of ideas, imageries, ideologies; and are as transitory and discontinuous as these, born afresh and vanishing without residual. The most formidable social phenomena, the very character of social relationships, the great social artefacts, the fearsome patterns of mass behaviour, the rules, codes and laws, the constitutions and the commandments − though they are engraved in stone − are, as Plato knew, no more than reflections of ideas and images weightless and without dimension. Such is the essential reality to which the statements of the sciences of society must ultimately refer. We know that this is so not only because of what we daily observe but also because of what we are; we who alone have access to the hidden source of our behaviour.

About that universe formed from the darkness and light projected from the mind's domain, there can be no general theory or statement that is universally and invariably true. There is no inherently determinant set of relationships nor any probability distribution that is inherently constant, continuous, consistent. And if statements made in the opening paragraph of this chapter, or any such statements about the social universe are sometimes so, they are sometimes no. They are true here, false there. Overwhelming us today, vanished tomorrow, improbable then, probable now. The tables of probability are as transient as the phenomena to which they refer.

Therefore no failure of a specific prediction of event or of probability can conceivably falsify general theory or generalizing statement in the social sciences.

QUALIFICATIONS

Nevertheless we very much need the general theory and generalizing statement about society to help comprehend this complex and changing universe of which we are a part. Nor does a discard of the notion of falsification through the test of specific prediction mean that the formulation of useful generalization and of credible general theory are not possible in the social sciences. On the contrary, we witness their existence and their consequences. There are long persisting regularities in the economy, in the polity and in society, enabling us with some success to generalize, to theorize and to predict. Nor does it mean that the theories and generalizations of social science need not or should not, through prediction, be submitted to the test of experience. But the predictions are of a special quality, without the right to be absolute and invariable, entitled to propose not a general truth but only what is generally true.

THE QUEST FOR ESSENCE

Whatever their methodological pretensions, the grand theories of Neo-Classical or Keynesian economics do not purport to explain anything in particular and for that reason they cannot be falsified by a failure to predict the particular. They assert 'tendencies', 'propensities', 'norms' (the marginal analysis for example), not true in every particular instance, possibly not true in any particular instance, but that would convey nevertheless the 'fundamental', the 'essential', contained within the flux and confusion of actual events.

It has been argued that generalizing statements in physics and in economics are both 'abstractions'. That is true; but they are abstractions of quite a different order. Compare for example the law of falling bodies in physics, with our famous Economic Man. Both generalizing statements, one with regard to physical and the other to social behaviour. Both abstractions. But the former conjectures a precise and specific relationship to be obtained in the absence of intervening variables, and to be tested through the removal or discounting of those variables. The latter while nowhere and never true claims nevertheless to describe a coherent pattern underlying the dispersion of events.

Taking into account the generalizing statements and the general theories that have been actually produced by the social sciences, and given a reference universe without determinant relationships or any inherently stable probability distribution, where the regularities that enable generalization are themselves a manifestation of human freedom in the choice and commitment to purpose and goal, we must conclude that the empirical discourse on general theory in the social sciences has never been and cannot be other than a quest for essence.

ANOTHER SORT OF JUDGMENT

But when theorists disagree? When claims to essence conflict? How shall we decide between them? Is the free market economy in capitalism the scene of harmonious interaction, interdependence, near to perfect efficiency, and mutuality of benefit, where each receives his/her just deserts? Or is it the scene of ruthless exploitation, irreconcilable contradictions and the carnage of class warfare? Instances of class conflict and exploitation and crisis can be found. Instances of harmonious interaction and mutuality of interests can be found. Which more credibly states the essence of things?

For the resolution such conflict, in spite of the injunctions of the canon, despite the imperative BE LIKE PHYSICS, there has been and there can be no other rational way than for the individual to weigh the evidence pro and the evidence con, and *judge* between them. Judgment, human judgment, individual judgment with all its fallibilities, is the key. There is no other that fits this lock.

We hear frequently of value judgments. But these are not judgments of values, but judgments of fact, judgment concerning an objective reality based on the empirical evidence pro and con. The statements of general theory in the social sciences are *empirico-judgmental* in contrast to the value-judgmental statements of moral philosophy and a normative discourse.

Recognizing this our task is to do what can be done to facilitate informed and clear-headed judgment.

IMPLICATIONS

Consider these other implications for economics and the other social sciences, where idea, image, ideology and values are at the core of social phenomena and event, that no general statement concerning their reference universe can have more than a transitory and limited claim to relevance and truth

Thus we might juxtapose E_1 (Neo-Classical Economics) and E_2 (Marxist Economics). Each of the two postulates or relies on a singular set of assumptions congruent with particular observations and experiences; and from these assumptions, each deduces an integral system that can claim to describe the whole operation of an economy. Besides E_1 and E_2, there might also be E_3, E_4, E_5, E_6, . . ., E_n: any number of other such integral systems, each based on a singular set of assumptions that derive from observation and experience and that can describe the whole operation of an economy. Which of these systems is the most relevant and revealing in relation to the events and phenomena with which *you* are concerned is, properly understood, a matter of judgment.

The test here is not whether the system is in accord with experienced reality, but with whether an experienced reality is in accord with the system. Falsification through the failure of specific prediction can occur only when conditions are fully in accord with the assumptions of the system, indicating then either that the theoretical structure interior to the system is logically deficient or that its initial specifications are incomplete. This must be the logic of Milton Friedman's position reviewed in Part 3 of Chapter 3 above, that all that can be properly questioned about an hypothesis is 'whether the hypothesis works for the phenomena it purports to explain'.

A particular failure of prediction does not falsify a system but rather marks out the boundaries of its relevance. So long as conditions somewhere actually or even potentially conform to the assumptions of a system, to that degree the system retains its relevance and credibility. This serves to explain the durability of E_1 and E_2 in the face of revolutionary change in their reference universe. Neither system is in error. The error is in their proponent's false claim to a universal credibility for the statements of their system, even in the face of a radical shrinkage in its boundaries of relevance.

6

General Theory: An Empirico-Judgmental Discourse

In some respects general theory in social science approximates the philosopher's model of science. As in the model, the theory has the demonstrated capacity to make significant generalizations: empirical generalizations about observable reality, that, because they are about the world out there, can be tested by reference to our shared experience: tested, directly or through inferential prediction. Having been made and tested, such statements sometimes fail the test. They are in Popper's terms, falsified. What the statement inferred need not occur. What the statement denied, may happen. In these respects the generalizing theory of the social sciences is like the philosopher's model of science.

There are also differences, setting generalizing theory in the social sciences apart from the philosopher's model of science. The basic difference has to do with the character of social relationships, compared to the relationships with which classical physics had to deal. The latter are determinant. The social relationships to which the general statements of social science refer are radically indeterminant, with neither constancy nor continuity in causal relationships nor in probability relationships. In the social universe, where freedom prevails and where encountered realities embody the transient ideas, imageries, ideologies, of the mind, what is true today may be false tomorrow; what is true here may be false there; what is here today is gone without a remnant or trace tomorrow; inconceivable today and pre-eminent tomorrow.

In spite of this radical indeterminance, temporally significant generalizations have been made by the social sciences; generalizations that have enabled societies to cope with their crises, and individuals to comprehend and to deal constructively with society, even though, in the instance of specific predictions, those generalizations are always and at once being verified and falsified.

Those who have looked for truth in the realm of general theory have not sought the unfalsifiable. In that realm the unfalsifiable is a chimera. They have sought the 'fundamental', the 'underlying', the 'tendential', the 'propensity'. the 'proclivity', the 'essential'. In fact and inevitably, theirs has been a quest for essences: essences like those of the philosopher. And the social scientists, seekers after essence, are as likely to imagine that what they find and what they offer is as pure and perpetual a truth as Plato thought his essences to be.

Invulnerable to falsification through prediction, claiming to themselves the fundamental, underlying, tendential truth of essences: nothing differentiates these general statements of social science from the statements of social philosophy. But to call them social philosophy does not answer the questions that concern us. For though philosophy would impose an iron rule on the conduct of science, it is quite silent concerning the conduct of philosophy. What method? what criterion of credibility? for the empirical generalizations of social science remains our question and dilemma.

There is an underlying truth of things as perceived by a line of thinkers from Adam Smith through Alfred Marshall to Milton Friedman. There is an underlying truth as perceived by Karl Marx and his followers. Both of these general theories are frequently, continuously falsified via the test of specific prediction. Both shrug off such falsifications as no disproof of the underlying, the fundamental, the tendential truth that they convey. Each dictates a totally different political posture and policy. How shall we choose between them?

A great problem is that each of them is not only a general statement about the world. It is also (like every paradigm) a mode of perceiving reality. And those inculcated into its mysteries will see and select out that which conforms with their preconceptions and will reject and ignore that which does not.

But for you and I who are not committed, how shall we know wherein lies the truth? How shall we choose the one as credible, or as more credible than the other? It must be said again: the best we can do is to know the facts including the facts of falsifications, and to weigh the evidence pro and con. There will always be evidence pro and evidence con. And then judge between them. To *judge* is the key.

The exercise of judgment leaves much to be desired as a way of establishing credibility. It allows for no definitive resolution of conflict and controversy. Extraneous values are likely to enter the process and corrupt the search for truth. Insulated as they are from definitive falsification, embedded in prejudice and re-enforced by the habituated mode of perception, empirico-judgmental statements are terribly difficult to dislodge. Nor can we answer the question: whose judgment should prevail?

It is therefore easy to understand why the philosophers of science should glory in the image of a discourse where credibility can always be established and conflict can always be resolved through the test of inferential prediction. If one could choose, one would always choose such a discourse. But for generalizing theory in the social sciences there is no choice. Its discourse must be empirico-judgmental because social phenomena are what they are. There is no option than to make credibility a matter of judgment, and judgment has its problems.

This argument has the following implications for practice and organization in the social sciences:

1. Most importantly it would urge an awakened awareness of the fragility and temporal character of general

statement in the social sciences, and of the role of judgment in establishing their credibility; a judgment that is the right and responsibility of every individual, and, given the transitory character of social realities, a judgment that should be renewed by every generation.

2.   Our great model for a system of social judgment is not science but the courts and their processes of counter-advocacy before judge and jurors. Can social science in some way follow this example, in legitimizing and promoting challenge and criticism, building these into the core of the discourse in order to keep judgment fresh and the facts of failure and contradication before the bar of opinion? For in the emprico-judgmental discourse, controversy should be the norm and no statement should cease to be questioned.

3.   If better judgment is the aim then the empirico-judgmental discourse must be organized to facilitate the ingathering and objective examination of the evidence, disciplined to minimize the intrusion of covert bias, with statements framed so as to allow the most complete exposure possible of the statement to the light of experience and as to enable the continuous comparison and contrast of the statement with the realities it claims to represent.

4.   In general the purpose of method and of rule should be that of facilitating a continuum of well informed, clear-headed judgment.

In that light we turn to an important question: what is the appropriate form of language for the the discourse on general theory in the social science?

7

The Mathematization of Empirico-Judgmental Discourse

The most distinctive change in economics and to a lesser degree in the other social sciences during the past half century, has been the mathematization of its language. This has been, we will argue, a crippling aberration that:

(1) fails its purpose,
(2) excludes a vital dimension of social phenomena from analysis,
(3) perverts the process of judgment in a discourse where, necessarily, credibility derives from individual judgment.

THE HYPOTHESIS FALSIFIED

In his doctoral dissertation of the late 1930s, which later became *The Foundations of Economic Analysis* (Cambridge, Harvard University Press, 1947), Paul Samuelson, in accord with the philosophers' admonition to BE LIKE PHYSICS, translated the established corpus of economic thought and theory from its verbal form into the mathematical sign. In so doing he staked out a path to be followed by post-war generations. The language of social science was transformed and some of its practitioners gained a mathematical virtuosity that is the envy of physicists.

Samuelson's purpose, as he wrote in the Foundations, was to open the statements of general theory to definitive test and falsification through inferential prediction. Implicit was this hypothesis. With its language transformed, propositions in economics would be tested and falsified through the failure of specific prediction, eliminating falsehood and clearing the way (as the canon promises) for the progress of the economic science towards greater truth. It was a test that never came. Not a single hypothesis in the corpus of established thought was ever subjected to the test of inferential prediction, falsified and eliminated. Accepting Samuelson's as its purpose, the great transformation in the nature of its language, the transformation failed that purpose. It did not work.

Though it failed in its purpose, the mathematization of economics was welcomed nevertheless, without reservation and for its own sake. And no one thought to test the consequence of the innovation against the purpose for which it was installed. Welcomed perhaps because it gave a new protective cover and a new prestige in the eyes of the uninitiated.

Mathematization ushered in an era of unprecedented growth and prosperity for the profession of economics, and of unprecedented sterility in the development of its substantive thought. That sterility, I will argue, was at least in part a consequence of mathematizing the language.

THE EXCLUSION OF THE QUALITATIVE: GEORGESCU-ROEGEN'S ARGUMENT

Nicholas Georgescu-Roegen, himself a world-famous econometrician, attacks the mathematizing of economics as having excluded qualitative difference, qualitative change and the emergence of novelty from the analysis of social behaviour.

With mathematics, he argues, physics could build upon the base of a relatively few central propositions, an immense system of statements descriptive of and able to predict observable phenomena. The viability of the instrument depends, however, on whether the character of the phenomena to be studied and the problems at issue can be encompassed by, or accommodated to, the symbolic structure of mathematics. For classical mechanics this was feasible inasmuch as:

(1) functional relationships are reversible,
(2) qualitative variability and evolutionary change need not be taken into account,
(3) the phenomena analysed are subject to cardinal measurement, that is, reducible to entities 'discreetly distinct as a single number in relation to the infinity of all others'.[1]

The truly vital elements of human behaviour, of economic process and of social organizations do not meet these preconditions and cannot be so encompassed by or accommodated to the symbolic structure of mathematics. The constituent elements of the economic process (wants, tastes, needs, motivations, identity, commitment, rationality, dedication, belief) are qualitatively variable. They are not 'discreetly distinct as a single number' and, hence, they are not subject to cardinal measurement. They are inherently ambiguous 'dialectical concepts'. The economic process is irreversible, enmeshed in historical time (and historical time has no mathematical analogue), its elements changing character and form with the emergence of novelty. All this is outside the scope of mechanism and mathematics. The economist's commitment to mechanistic model building and mathematical form forces the exclusion of the most essential constituents of human behaviour and social organization from analysis and concern.[2]

This he calls the 'arithmomorphism' of economic theory, a fallacious imitation of physics that destroys the relation between statement and experience.[3]

Through the triumph of classical physics, human knowledge escaped the strictures of animism, escaped, that is, from the projection of human experience onto the conceptualization and explanation of natural phenomena. The reverse metaphor, equally obscurantist, is now enthroned — a 'physicism' projecting a language and a mode of conceptualization proper to physics onto the study of man and of social organization.[4]

In sum, where and inasmuch as the language of economics and the social sciences are mathematized, qualitative variation, qualitative change, and all evolutionary processes and creative developments are *ipso facto* eliminated from consideration, accounting in good part for the inability of establishment economics to throw any light on the processes of innovative change and technological progress, and its feeble value in the analysis of economic development.

IN PRAISE OF MATHEMATICS

Consider these two systems of signs: the symbolic and the verbal, mathematics and the word. The critical attribute of mathematics in a system of discourse is that it abstracts from sensual experience. It is potentially without a residue of the observed and the felt. Nor need it convey any idea deriving from or referring to an observed, an observable, or a fancied reality. While the language of mathematics can be hooked into anything, it is about no thing. Our $2 + 2 = 4$ could refer to Bill and Jane, or to Jim and Mary, or to apples, or to nations, or to corporations, or to galaxies, but, *qua* language, it does not convey the idea or image of any of these. It is image-free, image-less. It is this attribute precisely that gives to mathematics its peculiar strength and value. Because it is purged of those equivocal and only partially communicable imageries attached to the word, mathematics and mathematics alone can convey the same meaning to all. Because it is free from the inherent imprecision of the sensed and observed, mathematics alone can express itself precisely. Because it is potentially detached from sensual experience and does not operate through a mental replication of events as they might be observed and grasped through the senses, mathematics can express the simultaneity of complex operations that words, always earthbound, cannot.[5]

Surely mathematics is unmatched as a means of exploring the inferential implications of statement through vectoring a matrix of simultaneous relations into the precise prediction of specific event. Which is to say that it perfectly suits the objective of experiment in physics. No other system of communication can so well chart distant inferences over the horizons of possible consequences, thereby both explaining phenomena and, through inferential prediction, testing the credibility or establishing the limitations of what is said. When, as in physics, it is not necessary to convey an image of the signified realities in order to establish credibility, indeed when there is no image to convey since the signified processes are hidden and made manifest only at the pin point of experienced event, then surely mathematics is the preferred language of discourse.

There are physicists who will think this statement goes overboard in its praise of mathematics. Perhaps they are right. But I want no quarrel with those who glory in the virtues of mathematics. I concede them every point. I do not at all dispute that mathematics is the appropriate language of 'scientific' discourse as Popper used the term, and hence where the credibility of statement can best be tested through a range of precise and specific inferential predictions.

IN THE EMPIRICO-JUDGMENTAL DISCOURSE?

But what value has mathematics in the empirico-judgmental discourse where, as in the case of general theory in economics, the credibility of statement cannot be based on the specific inferential prediction, but where the only rational path to credibility is through the individual judgment of a mixed bag of evidence pro and con? There the case for the mathematization of statement collapses.

This is not an attack on the use of numbers and measures. Systematic quantification, the use of numbers and quantity, the statistical gathering, questioning, correlating and arranging of data in comparing and evaluating economic performance or in otherwise providing the solid evidence needed for informed judgments, is of indubitable and inestimable value. Nor have we any quarrel with those who would employ mathematics as a private mode of thought. Our concern is with the capacity of the verbal statement in contrast to the symbolic sign to facilitate the judgment of generalizing statement about the universe of social behaviour and event.

Alfred Marshall the great British economist whose Principles written a century ago, has never been equalled as an expression of Neo Classical thought, was also a fine mathematician. But he abjured mathematics in the expression of his arguments because, he said, he wanted them understood by businessmen. It is a phrase that sounds rather quaint to us. But in his time and place, it signalled:

(1)   that economics is a policy science that must be understood and activated by those who govern relevant policy; in his time that was businessmen; hence

(2)   the acceptance of economic statement as the basis of policy was a matter for their judgment, and

(3)   that judgment required a verbal statement of his arguments.

But one must go further than Marshall. The verbal is not to be understood as a vulgarization or a simplification of the mathematical, but as having a fundamentally different character. And wherever judgment is at issue, it is the preferred instrument of communication.

The task of judgment is to understand and compare statement with the reality to which the statement refers. You tell me she is tall, blond and willowy. He says she is short and brunette. I must look and compare the stated image with the observed reality, and judge for myself. There is no way to convey the image which is of necessity the basis of judgment, save through the word.

If mathematics is imageless, purged of the imprint of the senses, the word in natural language is image-full and sense related. Natural language operates through replicating, recalling, conjuring up images in proxy of direct experience. It follows the earthbound sequence of sensual impression. Word follows word, image follows image, just as for the individual observation must follow observation. Word and observation alike are sluggard and unidimensional compared to the simultaneities in the free flights of logic open to mathematical expression. The word is equivocal because the image it summons in your mind and mine, are never identical. The word is imprecise because the imprint of experience, vague and fleeting or rich and deep, blurs at its margins and disintegrates in the microview.

The word, nevertheless, can do what mathematics can never do. It alone creates in the minds of communicants, speaker and spoken to, writer and written for, an idea of the experienced reality that is spoken about. As a reflection and replication of experience, the verbal expression alone conveys an image in the mind that can be checked against the observed and experienced, so that thought can be juxtaposed to observation, so that statement can be compared to experience directly, so that the stated and the observed — what is claimed and what is experienced — can be balanced on the same scale of judgment.

Only through verbal statement is it possible to create, bit by bit, in the minds of those to whom the word is spoken or written, a complex image of what is spoken or written about, so that it can be recognized and its untruth challenged through the realities of encounter. Only verbal statement conveys a meaning capable of being judged against the mixed evidence of experience. A statement made in the image-free symbolism of mathematics cannot of itself convey an idea of what is to be looked for. It cannot offer an image of the real, with this admonition: see for yourself; from what you have experienced, from what you have observed in the world of encounter, judge for yourself.

Following Popper's rule, in a universe of determinant relationships, all that matters for verification or refutation is that inferential prediction is on target. The language of statement is immaterial so long as it can extend deduction to an exact and certain end point. But in a universe in flux and transformation where relationships are inherently transitory and indeterminant, where contradiction and inconsistency abound and there is a pro for every con, it is judgment rather than the targeting of inferential prediction that counts for credibility. A statement that would capture the essence of things, must be image-full, in terms that mirror and can be reflected back on the universe of experience.

The verb is the instrument of individual judgment. To judge requires an image of that which is to be judged; an image that can only be conveyed through verbal discourse. Nor is that which is imaged by social science outside the scope of common observation. In a policy science in a democratic society moreover, statement should be grist for the judgment of the common man. Inasmuch as the image of the signified is hidden in the abracadabra of image-less mathematics, judgment on the credibility of empirical statement becomes impossible. Mathematization closes the door on the only rational way of establishing or challenging the credibility of general statement. Thus mathematization helps explain a substantive sterility without precedent in the development of post Second World War economics.

This chapter demonstrates that the mathematization of language in the general theory of economics and the social sciences:

(1) Is without 'scientific' justification or value.
(2) Eliminates any consideration of qualitative difference and of qualitative change, hence bars the effective analysis of technological advance, evolutionary change

and economic development at the heart of the modern economy.

(3) For judgment, the image of the subject to be judged must be conveyed in its fullness, which can only be done through the word. A methodology to enable informed, clear-headed judgment in an empirico-judgmental discourse, would give priority to the word. It would be for verbal statement to convey a clear image of the subject of analysis, with mathematics held to a supportive, service role.

8

Normative Theory and Other Components of Political Economy

THE VALUE-JUDGMENTAL DISCOURSE

We have differentiated, according to the character of their statement, the areas of discourse pertinent to the policy sciences. In the first instance, our emphasis has been on empirico-judgmental discourse about conceivably experienced phenomena and event, where a statement's claim to credibility must rely on a personal judgment of the evidence pro and con.

An understanding of social reality is always necessary but it is never enough for the rational formation of policy. Goals must be chosen, conflicts of interest must be resolved, oppositions brought into balance always by reference to criteria of right/wrong, better/worse, benefit/cost. All this belongs to another category of statement

Our question is not whether values are discussed and value- based generalizations are made. Of course they are. It is rather whether a disciplined discourse geared to the development of value-based systems of thought and criteria of choice for the formation of policy, should be developed as a part of the political economy. Because, in contrast to the empirico-judgmental, it must be based on value judgments, such a discourse might be called value-judgmental.

THE PURGE

Until the end of the 1930s, economics enjoyed the systematic coupling of its general theory and the moral philosophy of utilitarianism. Utilitarianism postulated a positive, pleasurable psychic response to the possession or consumption of marketed goods and services. That positive response, called utility, was attributed to the good or service possessed or consumed. It was further supposed:

(1) that such utility could be added to or subtracted from the sum of private satisfactions, e.g.,that three good meals give more utility than a single one, that a trip to Spain and then a trip to Italy gives more utility than a trip to Spain alone;

(2) that the utility attributable to the possession or consumption of an additional unit of A relative to that attributable to an additional unit of B is reflected in the individual's willingness to pay more for A than for B;

(3) that for a set of items possessed or consumed in series, the utility per item diminishes at the margin so that the fourth apple eaten in a row has less utility than the third, and, by derivation, that the utility attributable to increments of income or wealth also diminishes at the margin;

(4) and that in general, at a given level of income, the utility to be derived from an additional dollar of income or unit of consumption by one individual is comparable to that derivable under the same circumstances by another; hence that the shift of income from the richer to the poorer would increase the sum total of utility enjoyed by a society.

In the 1930s utilitarianism succumbed to positivist attack. John Hicks led the assault[1] calling Anathema on all that was not 'scientific' and decrying as 'unscientific' the utilitarian ethic at the roots of the discipline, and also the comparison of the satisfaction derived by an individual from an act of consumption with the satisfaction derived by another individual from the same act (or level) of consumption.

On that account henceforth, all value judgments, and all interpersonal comparisons were to be forbidden and purged from the discourse. This was a most curious critique, and I have never understood the gullibility of economists who swallowed it whole.

There is in fact nothing unscientific about interpersonal comparisons. To bar them on that or on any other grounds would put an end to such sciences as virology, immunology, psychology, epidemiology, comparative anatomy, and theories of disease.

The statement that utility exists as a common and comparable psychic response, that it is additive and that it decreases at the margin is an assertion of fact. It may be true or it may be false; certainly it is not a value judgment. Value judgment comes into play only with the assertion that society should seek to increase the happiness (satisfactions, utilities) of the people. And this value judgment is not one that Hicks shys away from. Rather, as we shall see, he reaffirms it.

In order to keep Neo-Classical thought more or less intact, while cutting general theory loose from its utilitarian roots, Hicks substituted the notion of preference for that of utility: e.g., For Mr Smith A has twice the utility of B = Smith is indifferent as between having one of A or two of B. The latter relationship is described as an indifference curve. Consumer behaviour is taken as the market expression of the indifference curves presumed as pre-inscribed in the psyche of each individual consumer.

What is the consequence of all this?

For the utilitarian hypothesis, another has been substituted concerning the psychic response of consumers to the possession or consumption of goods and services. The utilitarian hypothesis appealed to individual introspection and was consistent with the observed behaviour of consumers. The new hypothesis postulates an infinity of indifference curves, encompassing all conceivable combinations of that which could possibly be consumed and/or possessed at all possible levels of income, precisely incised in the individual psyche. It is a fantastic *melange* quite beyond the reach of introspection let alone any objective measurement. Its only support is in the notion that if Mr A buys *b*. rather than *c, d, e, f,* then *at least* it can be said that he must prefer *b* to *c, d, e* or *f*. But A's behaviour demonstrates nothing of the sort. Mr A might have purchased *b* because he is an automaton preprogrammed to buy *b* and nothing but *b*. (Try to disprove that without the use of interpersonal comparison!). Or Mr A could have bought *b* because he was told to, by his stockbroker, by his boss, by his wife, by his children, by his Aunt Matilda, and especially by that television commercial. He might have bought *b* in simple imitation of his neighbours. He might buy *b* knowing nothing about *c, d, e,* or *f*; indeed without knowing anything about *b* either. His purchase might be as random as when he buys a numbered lottery ticket or bets on the throw of the dice. The indifference analysis makes no attempt to explain whence came the preferences it assumes. To explain why *a* is preferred to *b*, one is driven back to something like the notion of utility.

Besides this substitution of a less credible for a more credible hypothesis concerning the psychic response of the consumer, the single 'achievement' of this indifference analysis was to forbid the economist *qua* economist to take any positive position with respect to income redistribution; forbidden to say, for example, that giving a loaf of bread to a starving child adds more to the sum of human happiness (satisfaction, utility) than the same loaf would have added to the sum of human happiness (satisfaction, utility) if offered to an overfed, slumbering multi-millionaire. Not that Hicks and his followers were against a positive stand in favour of more happiness. Under their curious rule of Pareto Optimality, the economist was urged to promote policies that would increase incomes and therefore add to the sum of happiness, satisfaction, utility, so long as no redistribution of income was at issue. In this Mr Hicks and his followers made not one but two value judgments: thou shalt give no consideration to income redistribution, and thou shalt support polices that will raise the level of income without redistribution.

There is no making sense of this charade on grounds of reason and truth. But there was, however, a quite practical explanation for what happened. The utility calculus leads to the conclusion, other things being equal, that the sum of human happiness, satisfaction or utility will be the greater the more equally that income is distributed, and that the sum of society's happiness, satisfaction or utilities will be less, the less equal is the distribution of income, and that happiness, satisfaction and utilities will be greatest when income is distributed equally to all.

To assert, under the sanction of science, that it is good to take from the rich and to give to the poor was not a message welcomed by the rich and powerful during those troubled decades of the 1920s and 1930s when revolutionary undercurrents ran strong on the continent of Europe and when in Great Britain there was for the first time the genuine threat that a Labour Government would assume power and make good on its perennial pledge to redistribute wealth. That that message should come from Neo-Classical text, would have seemed indeed a betrayal to the wealthy patrons of the discipline for long bastion of *laissez-faire* and supporter of the status quo.

In any case, a policy for the redistribution of income, finally possible, was hotly debated and fiercely controversial. And if the substitution of an indifference analysis did not eliminate value judgments nor interpersonal comparisons, it gave economics an escape hatch from that controversy. It restored the discipline's ideological bias. It preserved the goodwill of its patrons. For that John Hicks would be knighted and later receive the Nobel Prize.

There followed tortured decades of futile efforts to bring forth a Welfare Economics free of value judgment. It was foredoomed of course since without some value criterion it is impossible to distinguish welfare from illfare. Utility went underground, to reappear in one guise or another to prove the value of equality when income distribution was the issue. Thus John Rawls's widely applauded *Theory of Justice* (Cambridge, Harvard University Press, 1971) proposes an imaginary experiment. Unborn souls not knowing in whom they would be incarnated or with what facilities they would be endowed are asked whether they would prefer a more or less equal income distribution in the world that awaits them. With the spectre of diminishing marginal return floating in the background, it is assumed that pure self-interest would induce them to come down on the side of greater equality. That imaginary polling of unborn souls is supposed to legitimate the utilitarian argument for income equality, though how this eludes the necessity of a value judgment remains for me a mystery. The initial enthusiasm of economists for Rawls's theory suggests a craving for some legitimatized value criterion.

THE NATURE OF THE VALUE IMPERATIVE

Any normative discourse, utilitarianism for example, or Pigovian welfare economics,[2] will require a background of empirico-judgmental generalizations in order to predict the consequences of value-based options in the formation and implementation of policy.

But even the pure value imperative will have a certain resemblance to the empirico-judgmental statement. Like the latter the value imperative is capable of large encompassing generalizations: the Ten Commandments for example. Like the empirico-judgmental, the credibility or acceptability of the value statement requires and depends upon individual judgment. And the acceptability or credibility of the value-judgmental statement will depend on whether or not it resonates with the individual's experience.

The value-judgmental is, nevertheless, in fundamental respects different from the empirico-judgmental. The value-judgmental is not a conjecture about that which exists. It is not an hypothesis about experienced reality. It asserts an obligation, a moral command. Hence it allows of no inferential prediction or falsification through the failure of prediction.

Consider the Commandment: Thou Shalt Not Kill. We accept it, if we do, because we share an inner sense of the horror of killing and of being killed, which is based on our own experience and imagination, and what we know of the experience of others. But no prediction can be inferred from the Commandment: Thou Shalt Not Kill. Hence there can be no evidence of falsity through the failure of prediction. For the empirico-judgmental the subjective is brought to bear in comprehending and assessing objective experience. For the value-judgmental the objective experience is brought to bear in shaping the subjective, where the evidence pro and con counts only inasmuch as it effects our inner feeling.

THE ROLE OF A VALUE-JUDGMENTAL DISCOURSE IN ECONOMICS

Arguably no disciplined value-judgmental discourse is needed in political economy since, in any case, values relevant to policy choice are constantly being formed, reformed, transformed in the normal flux of social experience. Granting that, a value-judgmental discourse particular to the political economy could be useful in a number of ways.

It could drive value imperatives out of hiding, into the open, where we could know who stands for what, when and where. Better that values be brought to the surface than hidden, better overt than covert. To be aware of one's own, or of the discipline's understructure of value, to know the boundaries of moral commitment, is itself a value and a viable goal.

It could open policy science to an awareness of the real character and limitations of a normative discourse; at once of the absolute necessity of the value-judgmental in a policy science, and also the vulnerability of its claim to acceptability; and the realization that, in a rationally organized normative discourse, no value-judgmental statement stands as authorized and authoritative, and none are forbidden.

It could serve to discover the common denominator of moral commitment and to hammer out the consensus required for effective public action. Where the smaller reform is preferred to no reform, some strength to impotence, then such a discourse, through re-evaluation, adjustment and compromise, could enable those so engaged to find a common moral ground as a base for common action.

It could provide a forum where value-judgmental statement, can be creatively formulated, propounded, challenged, critiqued; and where value alternatives and alternative value-based systems can be contrasted and compared.

It could serve to explore and explain the moral consequences of empirical change, and the empirical consequences of a value imperative so that judgment on both counts might be better informed.

Philosophers philosophizing ask the question: 'What is the good.' Theirs has been the attempt to construct from a set of moral axioms, an encompassing system as a general guide to choice. For the empirico-judgmental discourse in the social sciences, the better question is in the order: 'What is a better mode of taxation? of police protection? of education? of energy conservation? of labour management relations? of conflict resolution?' The philosophers start at the base and build a system. It is for us to bring together the elements of the experienced and the potential into a living image of what could be. Theirs starts with a first judgment, ours with the final one. Hold up the image: this is what is possible. Take it as a goal. Choose it because you like the looks of it, for itself, as an end in itself, as a way to live. We need utopias to capture the imagination, to mobilize commitment to the concrete possibility that seems to us good.

We do not begin with a clean slate. We are born into a cultural system. We bear the imprint of its values. And it is at least the task of the present generation to reinterpret that heritage of values in the light of changes that have occurred in the character of society and in the problems it faces. We say that we believe in love, in justice, in equality, in equity, in the rights of man. What concrete meaning should be given to these avowals? How might they be embodied in the law? in institutions? in practice within the ever-changing circumstances of the here and now?. The following will exemplify the need for, and the adaptation of, moral commitment to change in the social context.

The Constitution of the United States guarantees the 'rights' of its citizens. What those who wrote the Constitution meant by 'rights' was space for the autonomous choice of the individual, to be preserved through the protected possession of private property and the prerogatives thereof, and through the political guarantees incorporated into the Bill of Rights. These were the rights valued and demanded in a society of self-sufficient, independent craftsmen-proprietors and farmers, in an economy of person-to-person exchange. With the drift of time, however, American society and its economy were fundamentally transformed. Industrialization, urbanization, the massive concentration of business enterprise, made the individual hostage to forces beyond his ken or control, and in response came the demand for rights of a different order: welfare rights and social guarantees against those imponderable insecurities and uncertitudes of modern life not imagined in the age of the Founders. Ours moreover is a society of organizations. Autonomy resides in the organization rather than in the individual. The individual occupies a niche in the organization and that niche determines his role, opportunities, privileges, protections, and powers. Hence the demand for, the need to formulate and institutionalize yet another set of 'organizational' rights: rights of the individual to share in the formation of organizational policy; rights and obligation attaching to organizational roles; rights to be protected against the arbitrary exercise of organizational power; rights against discriminatory barriers blocking individual entry into the preferred niches of the systems.

Or, to illustrate the way in which changed circumstances create a new moral challenge and the need to create new value criteria, consider the consequence of our failure to achieve full employment and price stability. I would argue that full employment and price stability is achievable, but only by combining Keynesian management of aggregate expenditure with price–wage control for the corporate organizational sector of the economy. I further predict that repeated failures will force policy along that path. Suppose I am correct in this. Then, via the control of prices and wages, the distribution of income would cease to be a random affair outside the reach of value judgment. It would become instead a matter of public choice and social policy. In order to establish in a democratic society a policy affecting income distribution, it would have to be accepted by the voting public as just and fair. By what criterion of justice and fairness to determine who gets what? The formation and establishment of an accepted value criterion as a basis for distributional policy (so-called 'incomes policy') is a critical and unfulfilled task for normative discourse.

Finally, and briefly, two other categories of statement that must be recognized as a part of the structure of a political economy.

IDEOLOGY

The normative and the empirical cannot stand apart in the process of policy formation. The empirical statement of that which is, imposes constraint and maps the topology to be traversed in order to reach the normative goal of that which ought to be. Wedded, the what is and the what ought to be, constitute an ideology. For the individual psyche and the cultural and cognitive systems of society, there is an immense complex of ideologies: ideas of what is and what ought to be for the family, for the church, for the work place, for the school, for the national defence, or in the sphere of economic policy, for social security, for taxation, for income redistribution, for national defence, for market competition, for corporate mergers, for the regulation of public utilities and so on.

It is to the grand ideologies, the 'isms' coupling general theory and universal goals, that the term 'ideology' usually refers. Creeds of Stalin, or of Mao, or of Hitler, or of Reagan and Thatcher, or of Khomeni enter the political process, as on to the field of battle in the struggle to contain and control a world of individual outlooks and of social choice. There, far from quietude of reasoned discourse, the battalions form. Mercenaries are recruited. Troops are mobilized into ranks where interests and values jostle. Zealots in the vanguard. Partisans find their identity in the ideological statement. Rather than to inform, rather than to reflect upon and consider, the word serves to proselytize, to propagandize, to arouse. And when the battle is joined, victory will be decided by the strength of emotional commitment rather than any proximity to truth.

The uncommitted in an effort at rational choice between ideological alternatives, have these options. They can return to the discourse on general theory to weigh the evidence in support of the empirical component of competing ideologies, and to the normative discourse to explore the implications of postulated goals and value-criteria. But also in this instance they can observe the political embodiments of ideologies acting on the stage of world event, to discern their effectiveness, their efficiency, their human consequences.

SOCIAL ENGINEERING

There is yet another area of discourse relevant to the political economy and to the rule of the public good. This is the neglected realm of the social engineer where, policy given, the question is as to ways and means. Here the criterion of choice is of effective implementation, cost reduction, workability. The task is creatively to develop technologies of political choice, of public accountability and control, of organization and management. Rather than the truths of its reference universe, it seeks the competence to deal with particulars, and to provide the tool-kit and the database for the formation of policy and its implementation.

Appendix

DISCOURSE AND STATEMENT

Here is science. What is it? What does the term signify? What does it mean in the specifics of concrete, everyday experience?

Certainly it is a set of statements, a complex body of statements pertaining to delimited realms of experience; statements that claim and *qua* science are accorded a high degree of credibility.

It is a system of discourse, global in scope, extendable in time. Since communication requires its avenues and its networks, since statement must be embodied in books and journals and organized as an archive, since the experiments necessary to explore realities and to establish the credibility of statement requires resources, since the inquiry, the experimentation, the reporting, the disputation, the communication, the learning all require time and effort and since those so engaged must be supported, science is also, necessarily, an organization and an operation with its policies and its programmes, its sanctions and its rewards, where resources must be allocated and power deployed.

And, as in any system of discourse where numerous individuals must communicate, share information, pursue common avenues of inquiry and dispute issues of common concern, science operates and must operate through some set of rules, overt and covert: rules of communicability, clarity, coherence, rules of authority, choice, verification.

THE NATURE OF STATEMENT

The element of all discourse is the statement. Argument, proposition, hypothesis, theory, datum, prediction: all are

119

stated. And in response comes the challenge, the question, the rebuttal, the correction, the elaboration: all stated. Statement upon statement weave the web of discourse.

What forms of statement could constitute the discourse of the sciences? Here, with the help of a formal device, we will try to give a rigorous answer to that question.

Following Ferdinand Saussure, founder of structuralist linguistics, we understand every statement as a sign. For every sign there are two constituents, the signifier, and the signified. The signifier is the formal, conventional, symbolic element: word, sentence, proposition, theory. It indicates. It points to. The signified is that which is pointed to and/or is pointed from. Here the signifier $= S$, and the signified $= s$. This relationship, with the signified/signifier on the one side and that which indicated on the other can be illustrated as shown in Figure 1.

$$\frac{s \text{ (signified)}}{S \text{ (signifier)}} \; = \; \text{TREE}$$

Figure 1

The signified then has a possibly dual existence. It must always exist as an image or some form of mental construct embedded in the psyche of the one who makes the statement as well as to the one who attempts to understand it. We denote this mental construct as s'. The referenced object, event, or condition, we denote as s. Hence s and s' are two meanings that attach to the signifier S. The signifier 'cat' signals both the grey object resting in the crook of my arm, and the image of the animal in the realm of your thought and mine.

The relationships between s' and s, and between S and s, and between S and s', constitute problem areas open to analysis.

The viability and limitations of the signifier S depends on its capacity to express and convey s and s'; which in turn determines the effectiveness of discourse. Hence a primary objective of socially organized, most particularly of education in science, must be to articulate and most firmly inculcate in the minds of the scientists the relationship between S and s/s' as absolute and universal, and the meaning of s and s' as explicit and clear. How else to maintain effective communication in a world-wide discourse where anyone is free to enter, but where each must understand the S, the s and the s' of another's statement.

This objective, imperative for effective discourse, of firmly imprinting in the minds of scientists a universal and inviolable sign that equates S and s' and s is also a trap for those engaged in the discourse of science, particularly in the social sciences, for, and, and especially in the social sciences, that which is signified, e.g., the economy, need not be constant but is, on the contrary, in a continuing state of change. But while the referenced object s changes and changes radically, the image of that which is signified s is too firmly inculcated to change. The clarity and universality of the sign, hence of the universality and unshakeability of the inculcated relationships s, s'/S as an imperative of scientific education can introduce a profound resistance to the recognition of contradiction between the signified and the actual.

The appropriate rules of discourse depend upon the character of statement. We will specify three categories of statement, defined by the relationship of signifier and signified, namely the tautological, the empirical and the expressive.

(1)   The tautological statement has no reference object. Hence s' does not appear in the equation. The signifier

is itself the signified. The tautological statement is a sign enclosed within itself. In the definition, in the equation, in the model, tautological statements are ubiquitous, essential, inescapable. Whenever the sign is verbal rather than symbolic, there will be an equivocal relation between S and s. The tautological statement can be repudiated as incoherent, inconsistent and incomplete, but whether verbal or symbolic, whether expressed in words or in numbers, it cannot be reached and challenged by experience or experiment.

(2)   The expressive statement expresses the psychic condition, the state of being, the feelings, the volition, the conviction of the one making the statement. The objective condition to which such a statement refers is specific to and within the observational scope only of the one who feels, wills, state, and cannot be observed in common by others who are parties to the discourse.

Laughter signalling 'I feel joy', or 'That's funny' or 'You're ridiculous', is an expressive statement. So are the words 'I love you', or 'I prefer brunettes'. The signifier S expresses and refers to the psychic state of the one who does the signifying. Hence $s' = s'/S$.

The expressive statement is no tautology. It refers to the experienced and the observable, but in a domain to which the one who signified has privileged entry. While what is described or referred to is experienced exclusively by the one making the statement, its signal or signifier S is open to common observation and falls into the domain of the empirical. Whoever listens may take another's laughter as an objective phenomenon. To comment, 'He is laughing', is as much a statement of empirical fact as any other. And though we cannot enter into and observe the condition of the psyche that his laughter expresses, we can and do make a deduction (He must think something is funny) concerning it. This raises the tricky issue of 'interpersonal comparisons'. I cannot enter the laughing man's psyche, but I deduce he thinks something is funny because I laugh when something seems funny to me.

In practice these forms of statement will meld together. Anyone making an empirical or a tautological statement will have a reason for making that statement, and that reason may enter into the statement, and the statement may express the inner reason, the motivating emotion that underlies the statement. To say 'My colleague is a low-down, lying, bastard', may be an empirical statement of fact, but who would deny its expressive overtone? To define capitalism as a system of organized thievery, is, like all definitions, tautological, but who would not see it as an expressive statement as well?

THE VALUE IMPERATIVE

Consider the statement:

> Granted I cannot be sure that your pleasure and your pain are just like mine, or that your unhappiness at being poor is equal to what I would suffer from a like deprivation. Even so I believe we should consider your pain and my pain from a given benefaction, as equal and the same. On that account the dollar loss and the dollar gain to each and every one of us should be given the same considera- tion, and our pain and pleasure should be weighed on the same scale.

Again an expressive statement. It expresses the subjective fact of my belief, my conviction. But with a difference. For it is framed as an imperative, as a statement of what ought to be, or what should be done. it is not of the order of 'I love you', but of 'Love thy neighbour as one who is as thyself'.

Such statements enter into discourse as 'value judgments'. I would prefer 'value imperatives'.

THE EMPIRICAL STATEMENT

We call statements about it out there, where that which is signified can be observed by us both if we care to look or otherwise made subject to a shared experience or testing, empirical. They are the prototype element of the discourse of science. In the empirical statement, the signifying image s' and the signifier S point to and are about s in the domain of shared or shareable experience. Hence where $s'/S = s$. This s, objective reference of an empirical statement, need not be quantifiable, measurable, recordable, or even visible. Thus for example, Neo-Classical economics is about consumer preferences. Marxist economics refers to the interests of social classes. Freudian psychoanalysis has to do with psychic trauma. Such phenomena as these, invisible and hidden in the inviolable domain of the individual psyche are an objective reference nevertheless, inferred from observed behaviour and expressive statement.

Notes

1 Confessions

1. The book did not appear in English until 1959, incorporated into *The Logic of Scientific Discovery* (Hutchinson, London).
2. An entirely trivial work that turns on the proposition that economics is the science of allocating scarce resources among alternative end uses. Certainly Neo-classical economics does postulate a particular system of resource allocation, but the definition would apply even more aptly to engineering or military science or other crafts and disciplines. On the other hand, portions of the corpus of economic thought, e.g., Keynesian or Malthusian theory, fall outside its definitional scope. Yet it earned Robbins an international reputation, perhaps because it made economists more secure in their status as 'scientists'.
3. At the time I had not yet read Schumpeter's *Capitalism, Socialism, and Democracy* (New York; Harper & Row, 1942). Therefore I did not realize that in that book Schumpeter had anticipated some of my arguments in what he called the 'routinization' of innovation.
4. Robert A. Solo 'Research and Development in the Synthetic Rubber Industry,' *Quarterly Journal of Economics*, February 1954; *Synthetic Rubber: A Case Study in Technological Development Under Public Direction* (Washington DC, GPO, 1961), reprinted as part of *Across the High Technology Threshold* (Wynwood, Pennsylvania, Norwood Press, 1980).
5. Footnoted below are some random samples of publications related to the roles and work experience indicated in the text.
6. Robert A. Solo, 'Creative Technology and Economic Growth', *International Development Review*, February 1961.
7. Robert A. Solo, 'Gearing Military R&D to Economic Growth', *Harvard Business Review*, November–December 1963.
8. Robert A Solo 'The Capacity to Assimilate and Advance Technology', *American Economic Review*, May 1966, and

Organizing Science for Technology Transfer in Economic Development (East Lansing, Michigan State University Press, 1975).

9. Robert A. Solo, 'Patent Policy for Government Sponsored Research and Development', *Idea*, Summer 1966.

10. Developed in my *Economic Organizations and Social Systems* (Indianapolis, Bobbs-Merrill, 1973).

2 Popper's Progress

1. . . . human opinion universally tends in the long run to a definite form, which is the truth. Let any human being have enough information and exert enough thought upon any question, and the result will be that he will arrive at a certain definite conclusion which is the same as any other mind will reach under sufficiently favorable circumstances. . . . There is then to every question a true answer, a final conclusion, to which the opinion of every man is constantly gravitating. He may for a time recede from it, but give him more experience and time for consideration, and he will finally approach it. The individual may not live to reach the truth; there is a residuum of error in every individual's opinions. No matter it remains that there is a definite opinion to which the mind of man is, on the whole and in the long run, tending. On many questions the final agreement is already reached, on all it will be reached if enough time is given. Charles Sanders Pierce, *Collected Papers*, Charles Hartshorne and Paul Weiss (eds) (Cambridge, Harvard University Press) par VIII, p. 12.

2. Schlipp, *The Philosophy of Karl Popper*, p. 1146.

3 Popper's Canon, Kuhn's Paradigm and Economics

1. Similarly Marxist economics expresses the same episteme and takes the same form as Darwinian biology in the nineteenth century.

2. In a footnote Keynes quotes Marshall, 'Just as the motion of every body in the solar system affects and is affected by every other, so it is with the elements of the political economy'.

3. Paul Samuelson, *The Foundations of Economic Analysis* (Cambridge, Harvard University Press, 1947).
4. John R. Hicks, *Value and Capital* (Oxford, Clarendon Press, 1946).
5. Edward H. Chamberlin, *The Theory of Monopolistic Competition* (Cambridge, Harvard University Press, 1962).
6. Joan Robinson, *The Economics of Imperfect Competition* (London, Macmillan, 1969).
7. Moses Abramovitz, 'Resource and Output Trends in the United States since 1870', *American Economic Review, Proceedings*, May 1956.
8. Solo, 'The Insignificance of Capital Accumulation', *Economic Organizations and Social Systems*, pp. 91–130.
9. Luigi Passinetti, 'On Concepts and Measures of Changes in Productivity', *The Review of Economics and Statistics*, August 1959, p. 270.
10. Robert M.Solow, 'Technical Change and the Aggregate Production Function', *The Review of Economics and Statistics*, Vol. 39, August 1957, pp. 312–20.
11. Roy Harrod 'Second Essay in Dynamic Development', *The Economic Journal*, June 1960.
13. Fritz Machlup, *Methodology of Economics and Other Social Sciences* (New York, Academic Press, 1978).
14. Donald McClosky, *The Rhetoric of Economics*, (Madison, Wisconsin, The University of Wisconsin Press, 1985).
15. Starting with Fritz Machlup, 'The Problem of Verification in Economics', *Southern Economic Journal*, July 1955, Tjalling C. Koopmans, *Three Essays on the State of Economic Science* (New York, McGraw Hill, 1957); K. Klappoholz and J. Agassi, 'Methodological Prescriptions in Economics', *Economica* Feb. 1959; the controversy took an interdisciplinary character and a national platform with Ernest Nagel's paper, 'Assumptions in Economic Theory', and discussion papers by Paul Samuelson and Herbert Simon on 'Problems of Methodology', *American Economic Review*, May 1963; followed by Fritz Machlup, 'Professor Samuelson on Theory and Realism', and Paul Samuelson, 'Theory and Realism: A Reply', *American Economic Review*, September 1964; Jack Melitz, 'Friedman and Machlup on the Significance of Testing Economic Assumptions', *Journal of Political Economy,* Feb.

1965; Abba P. Lerner, Gerald J. Massey and Gerald Garb in separate comments on 'Professor Samuelson on Theory and Realism' and Paul Samuelson's, 'A Reply', *American Economic Review*, December 1965; D. V. T Bear and Daniel Orr, 'Logic and Expediency in Economic Theorizing', *Journal of Political Economy*, April 1967; Lawrence Boland, 'Methodology as an Exercise in Economic Analysis', *Philosophy of Science*, March 1971; Stanley Wong, 'The F-Twist and the Methodology of Paul Samuelson', *American Economic Review*, June 1973; Charles K. Wibur and John D. Wiseman, 'The Chicago School: Positivism or Ideal Type', and Warren S. Gramm, 'Chicago Economics From Individualism True to Individualism False' both in Warren J. Samuels (ed.), *The Chicago School of Political Economy*, East Lansing, Association for Evolutionary Economics, 1976; Arthur Kemp, 'The Political Economy of Milton Friedman', *Modern Age*, Winter 1978; Lawrence Boland 'A Critique of Friedman's Critics', *Journal of Economic Literature*, June 1979, and 'On the Futility of Criticizing the Neo-Classical Maximization Hypothesis', *American Economic Review*, December 1981; William J. Frazier Jr. and Lawrence A. Boland, 'An Essay on the Foundations of Friedman's Methodology', *American Economic Review*, March 1983, and, no doubt other publications.

16.	'Taped Discussion with Milton Friedman', Stanford University, 6 Feb. 1979, reported by Frazier and Boland, 'An Essay on the Foundations of Friedman's Methodology'.

17.	Samuelson, 'Problems of Methodology', p. 233

18.	R. Hall and C. J. Hitch, 'Price Theory and Business Behavior', *Oxford Economic Papers*, May 1939; Committee on Price Determination, Conference on Price Research, *Cost Behavior and Price Policy* (New York, 1943); H. M. Oliver Jr., 'Marginal Theory and Business Behavior', *American Economic Review*, June 1947; R. A. Lester, 'Shortcomings of Marginal Analysis for Wage-Employment Problems', *American Economic Review*, March, 1946.

19.	He adds that the Alchian survival argument, i.e., if they were not profit maximizers they would not survive, 'does not help matters, since it, like Z, cannot be tested by direct observation — we cannot identify the profit maximizers' (p. 230).

4 Social Science, Policy Science

1. For a formal treatment of statement and its variations, see the Appendix.

7 The Mathematization of Empirico-Judgmental Discourse

1. N. Georgescu-Roegen, *The Entropy Law and the Economic Process* (Cambridge, Harvard University Press, 1971) p. 14.
2. Ibid., pp. 1–3 and *passim*.
3. Ibid., p. 99.
4. Ibid., p. 79.
5. This is illustrated in the instance of the Walrasian equations. These equations add nothing to our knowledge of reality. They have never been tested nor are they testable and falsifiable through prediction. Why then do some regard them as the high point of economic theory? Economics had long been committed to the idea of a general equilibrium wherein, through the free movement of price, all the elements of an economy are brought into a predetermined, predeterminable and stable point of balance. Except that the process of achieving a point of general equilibrium could not be expressed through our earthbound words, which could only describe the movement towards equilibrium in one market after another but not through the simultaneous movement of all markets acting and interacting upon each other. That needed mathematics. So, with prior theory as its empirical reference, the Walrasian equations demonstrated that the notion of general equilibrium can be concretely expressed.

8 Normative Theory and Other Components of Political Economy

1. John R. Hicks, *Value and Capital* (Oxford, Clarendon Press, 1946).
2. A. C. Pigou, *Economics of Welfare* 4th edition (London, Macmillan, 1932).

Index